Jane Williams was born in India ol
of five sisters. She took a degree in ...., ... and has
worked in theological publishing and in Christian adult education.
She is a Visiting Lecturer at King's College, London, and a tutor at
the St Paul's Theological Centre, London. Her publications include
Bread, Wine and Women (with Sue Dowell; Virago 1994), *Lectionary
Reflections, Years A, B and C* (SPCK 2003, 2004, 2005), *Approaching
Christmas* (Lion Hudson 2005), *Approaching Easter* (Lion Hudson
2006), and *Angels* (Lion Hudson 2006). She is married and has two
children.

MARRIAGE, MITRES AND BEING MYSELF

Jane Williams

First published in Great Britain in 2008

Society for Promoting Christian Knowledge
36 Causton Street
London SW1P 4ST

British Library Cataloguing-in-Publication Data
A catalogue record for this book is available from the British Library

ISBN 978-0-281-06018-4

1 3 5 7 9 10 8 6 4 2

Typeset by Graphicraft Ltd, Hong Kong
Printed in Great Britain by Ashford Colour Press

Produced on paper from sustainable forests

Contents

Contents

Introduction

In my travels around the Anglican Communion with my husband, I have become more and more impressed by bishops' spouses. The occasion for this book is the Lambeth Conference of 2008, where bishops from all over the Anglican world will meet to pray and try to discern God's will for this portion of his Church. Most of them will be accompanied by their spouses. Ironically, although my husband has been a bishop for a number of years, I have never been to a Lambeth Conference before: small children and a job have always prevented me in the past from wanting, or even being able, to spend three weeks in the British school summer holidays in the company of bishops and their spouses. So when I discovered that I would be expected to mastermind the spouses' conference this time, I was taken aback, and not completely sure that such a thing should happen, given the financial constraints of the Church today. But just a few years of meeting bishops' spouses has persuaded me.

It has become increasingly clear to me that the churches in which their episcopal spouses serve are deeply indebted to what the wives and husbands of bishops do. Some people are aware of that debt, but many are not, and simply take it for granted that it is a privilege to be married to a bishop.

Most of the people who have contributed the articles on which this book is based would agree that they are, indeed, very privileged. But they might well be defining the term rather differently from the way in which the average observer would, as we shall see.

In writing the book, I am faced with something of a dilemma. I want the reader to see the joy and the sense of purpose and the love of the Church that all of the contributors express. I want this book to be a celebration both of bishops' spouses and of the Church that they so willingly serve. But I also want to be truthful about the constraints, expectations and costs that some bear as part of being married to a bishop. If this were only to be read by other bishops' spouses, I could concentrate much more on the latter, and know that I would get wry smiles of recognition, and many more anecdotes from readers who had experienced similar situations. Any bishop's spouse who has had to bring up children in that kind of limelight has stories to tell, as has every bishop's spouse who has been left unrecognized at the back of a church while the bishop is being mobbed by enthusiastic churchgoers. Most episcopal spouses can tell stories about the miracles they have performed in the way of feeding the five thousand unexpectedly and with no money. Most have learned to smile and keep silent when hearing their spouses misrepresented and slandered.

But although these and many more are common experiences, recognized by all episcopal households, the underlying sense of privilege is also something that we all take for granted, and that all the contributors to this book expressed in one way or another. When we meet together, we don't always remember to talk about that side, but when we try to think about how we are seen by those who do not know the inside story, then the sense of being where God has called us to be, which is probably the most precious thing any believer can have, needs to be highlighted.

Because most bishops' spouses are not boat-rockers, great numbers of them kindly agreed to write briefly about their lives when I asked them to. If they thought it was a bad idea, on the whole, they just politely ignored the request, rather than writing or ringing or emailing to give me a piece of their minds. That is probably partly the result of years of episcopal training, rather than that all bishops' spouses are, by nature, peaceful non-complainers.

But one thing that many of them did express was a sense of continuing bewilderment that such a book should be of interest, and a slight suspicion that the interest might be prurient rather than genuinely seeking for information. All of us get asked, quite regularly, what it is like to be married to a bishop. And, of course, we can only reply that we have only ever been married to one bishop each, and that that is hardly a fair sample on which to give a general answer. Bishops and their spouses are as different as any other members of any other profession. But, on the whole, we are aware that the question comes from those who would like to pray for us better and support us better, and who love the Church and want to see its human faces with a smile on them.

I hope this book will give such kind readers an idea of the things that bishops' spouses have in common, as well as their individuality and variety. The book will look at the faith that underpins our lives, at the issues we face in living in such public homes, and at the effect on our families. It will also try to give some idea of what is required of the bishop's spouse when ministry is exercised in a war-torn area, or a place where it is not culturally acceptable to be a Christian.

All of these issues and many more will be on the table as we meet together at the Lambeth Conference. And while we will discuss and share expertise and try to equip ourselves better for God's calling upon our lives, we will also, I hope, celebrate God's Church and demonstrate why God has entrusted us with the good news of his love for the world – not because we are wonderful (although we are, rather), but because we are willing.

I thank all who have contributed to this book and all who have shared their stories with me verbally. I am proud to be one of that strange company of Anglican bishops' spouses.

Jane Williams

Wendy Pritchard
Jarrow (Durham Diocese, England; now Oxford, England), married to Rt Revd John Pritchard

At the moment, this involves working full time, arriving home tired and preparing a meal, washing up, then starting to make curtains and turn out drawers as we move in six weeks' time! Just like anyone else in that situation, I could do with four more hours in a day, or standard window sizes across the country!

In general, though, I've found being a bishop's wife in the north of England an immense privilege. People here are not obsessed by status, and treat everyone as an equal. I've been called 'pet' and hugged by total strangers, and been told intimate details of people's lives. I've been fascinated by the life stories of older women who have vivid memories of the times when the church was full and the whole community was involved there. I've been to a moving ceremony to remember those who lost their lives in a local pit disaster, then talked to people who could remember the miners coming home black with coal dust, and not being allowed into the house until they had washed outside in the yard.

I accompany my husband on a Sunday to whichever church he is visiting, so I have been to services in school halls, ancient buildings, our beautiful cathedral and even a supermarket car park. Each one has had its own character and has been made special by the devoted congregation who have given such love and care to maintaining their church. Some of the congregations are small, but they are all very welcoming. I feel it is a big responsibility to show these wonderful people how much they are appreciated and not to be a distant figure demanding some sort of special recognition. It is an important part of the role of the Bishop's wife to be approachable and interested – not a difficult thing to be!

Another part of the role is to welcome people into our home. I like cooking (although I am invariably on the last minute getting the food prepared) and to have a group of clergy round is a way of affirming them and showing them that they matter to us. Many have very difficult working situations, and deserve much recognition and encouragement.

I feel strongly that being a bishop's wife is a privilege and a gift, which needs to be seen positively. *God* has called us to this place and to our future – whatever it holds – and he is to be trusted.

Sorry not to write more, but I need to go and make curtains!

Barbara Packer
Ripon and Leeds (England), married to
Rt Revd John Packer

I think the first word that comes to mind is 'opportunity'. I do not often feel under pressure to fulfil particular roles as a bishop's wife, but there are many possibilities that open up. Some of these involve entertaining and hospitality. The opportunity to use the house and the role to bring together groups of clergy, head teachers, journalists, interfaith groups, etc. is rewarding both personally and in the opportunity for bridge-building which it provides. I often feel moved and humbled by the delight that people express at being invited to such an event. In many situations it is possible to convey to people that their work is valued, just by being there.

At Easter 2005, not long after the tsunami, we were able to visit our linked dioceses in Sri Lanka and the role opened up the possibility of making close contacts there with many people at the heart of the rehabilitation effort, including the bishops. Then, on returning home, because of people's awareness of our visit, I was able quickly and effectively to arrange visits to parishes to talk about what our partners are experiencing.

Other opportunities involve invitations to be present at formative moments in local and national history – be it the opening of an interfaith playgroup or a crucial moment in the House of Lords. I have also found myself being invited to join diocesan and other local organizations, initially because of my position. This can then become a ministry of my own. For instance I enjoy my role as vice-president of our diocesan Mothers' Union, and all that involves.

There is a 'down side' to all this. I found when I moved from vicarage to bishop's house that I lost the day-by-day close relationships of the parish, which I had greatly valued. There, too, we practised hospitality, and many groups met in our house, with the possibility of developing relationships. Now the groups I meet are more often unknown or slightly known to me. In visiting around the diocese and attending worship, too, I meet a huge number of people, often superficially. It requires a degree of extroversion that does not come naturally to me! The choice I have made to accompany John to different churches on Sundays also leaves me without a regular church to relate to, although I try to go to my local church about once a month.

This rootlessness is one reason why it is important to me to continue in my own profession: I have a half-time post as a teacher of maths to adults, and this is probably the part of my work that affirms my own identity and particular skills, and gives a rhythm to my weeks. The constraints of time and availability have meant that I have not been able to develop my career as I might otherwise have done, but this has been a price worth paying.

I think I am still relatively unusual in being a diocesan bishop's wife in paid employment. It is now true that the vast majority of spouses of parish clergy are in employment, but not many bishops' wives. I find this shared experience helpful in my relationships with clergy spouses in the diocese. I see it as part of my role to facilitate events for spouses, and to have a pastoral concern for them, along with 'spouses' links' in each deanery. This is all fairly 'light touch', as most clergy spouses now have other support systems and concerns, and are busy combining at least two roles.

I think I see my most important role as providing stability and support on a personal level for my husband, John. Inevitably his life can be stressful, with irregular and long hours, with a variety of intractable issues at different times, and I hope I can provide emotional as well as practical support. Often it is I who am able to attend our children's significant events, when John may not be free.

All in all, I regard the role as much more privilege than burden!

Rebecca Parsley
Alabama (USA), married to Rt Revd Henry Parsley

I like to think that the beginning of my life as a Christian was at baptism when I was an infant, and even before that if one considers that my parents were also Christians. As is typical of so many of those in my country whose ancestors came from other shores, they brought their religion with them, in my family's case from the shores of Great Britain. Since my mother's family were members of the Church of England, they soon became Episcopalians as this evolution had occurred rather early in America's young life. My father's family was from the Methodist tradition but my mother's Episcopal determination held in the end and thus we are an Episcopal family and to that I say, thanks be to God!

If one considers that becoming a Christian is the time that one consciously chooses and proclaims that one will follow Jesus and Christian principles, then I would identify the occasion of my confirmation at age 12 as the formal beginning of that process. I think growing up as an Episcopalian is a great privilege and I believe that I am still growing in faith. In fact, through every stage of life, the structure and teaching of the Church have guided me and provided a foundation through 'many dangers, toils and snares', as well as through a full measure of 'amazing grace'. How grateful I am for that foundation.

I was born in New Orleans, Louisiana, in 1951, the child of a physician and a ballet dancer. We also lived in St Louis, Missouri, and then in Jackson, Mississippi, during the civil rights years of crisis. I saw and heard much as a young girl, yet was guided by wise and compassionate parents and clergy. In the middle of the tumultuous 1960s we moved to New York City where I attended the United Nations International School and found myself among friends from around the world. As varied as were our cultures, religions and countries, we had the freedom to experience life together and enjoy each other without the worldly borders of politics, race, culture or religion. I have always considered that experience one of God's greatest blessings in my life. It was an epiphany to understand that we children, from nations around the globe occasionally on opposing sides of issues, could in fact live in love and charity with each other. It may have been a world seen through the eyes and naivety of a young person, yet it remains a source of great hope to me for our Church and country and for our world.

Henry and I met at the University of the South in Sewanee, Tennessee, and we married in the chapel there in 1970. After two years at General Seminary in New York, we moved to Oxford, England, for a course of study. Following his ordination in 1973, he served five churches in two dioceses and was consecrated bishop in 1996 in the Diocese of Alabama. It has long been a dedicated and generous diocese in the Church and we were thankful to make our home among these faithful people. At the time of his election, I was particularly grateful for having known the Church and having been a spouse of a priest in it for so many years. Becoming the spouse of a bishop was primarily an adjustment of focus for me. I found that my sense of responsibility and interests called me away from my former work in a bookstore and as an educator, to a new and exciting work with the clergy spouses in our diocese, with the spouses of bishops here and beyond and with Henry as we travel together throughout the Church. I have quite enjoyed being an active part of both spouse communities and have discovered a passion for outreach and mission work as we have established relationships with companion dioceses in Brazil and Haiti.

Introduction

My first experience at the Lambeth Conference in 1998 brought into focus the unique blessings we as spouses of bishops throughout the Anglican Communion have together and the inestimable gift we give each other when we share our stories and pray for and with each other each day as we live in community, a global community under one roof. We made many friends there with whom we still connect and for whom we are very thankful. If only for those short weeks, it is a marvellous gathering indeed. This experience prompted me to become an editor of our newsletter for spouses in the Episcopal Church in the USA (ECUSA) called *Pathways*, which links our own spouse community and often invites participation from spouses around the Anglican Communion.

Through our many connections with Anglicans around the world we now have what I like to call a community of 'friends without borders' who have in common an abiding love for Christ and the Church and for each other. How comforting that is as I look ahead to the future of our worldwide family of churches, where children can live and grow in grace knowing that there are millions of people who love and pray for them every week and break bread at the table of our Lord in communion with Anglicans everywhere.

There is much for which I give thanks and I give very special thanks indeed for our Church because through it we are invited to higher common ground in our life together every day, in our joys and in our sorrows, united by the profound love and grace of Jesus Christ. I believe it is that which defines who I am, and who we are together as Christians.

1

The winding road

Bronwyn Fryar, a bishop's wife from central Queensland, Australia, used the phrase 'the winding road' to describe her life. That is partly because, in Australia, dioceses are so huge that bishops inevitably spend a large amount of time on the road, as they do in Africa, too. 'The journeys are long but the car also offers space of both time and place, for conversation and company', as Bronwyn Fryar says. Space and time are both precious and often in short supply in the life of a bishop's family.

But the 'winding road' also describes the sense of expectation and surprise that many of the contributors expressed about their Christian journey. Not a single one of them remembered a childhood desire to be married to a bishop! 'No one expects the Spanish Inquisition!' Nara Duncan quotes, wryly. What is more, if their school friends had been asked to guess what profession they would marry into, almost none would have said 'the Church'. One bishop's wife recalls an old friend asking, 'How is it that the naughtiest girl in the school is a bishop's wife?' Another, Kathy Gregg from Eastern Oregon, says that she and her husband 'always laugh that I did so poorly in college religion classes only to marry a priest and a scholar'. Very few of them actually married a bishop, or even a priest. Most of them would have expected and even preferred a different path in life. But all of them walk with God, and they know that God's road has many corners, and that it is just no good trying to see around them until you come to them. I do not know if there are any Anglican bishops whose spouses do not believe in the Christian God and practise their faith. I can only say that I have not met any, and that I think the life would be almost impossible without that sense of walking with God in obedience and hope.

Many of the spouses who wrote for this book grew up in Christian families, though not all were Anglicans. Their journeys of faith were not untypical of stories that a cross-section of Christians of any kind would tell. Some started off as merely dutiful church-goers and gave it up for a bit when they left home. Some cannot remember a time when they did not believe. Some have struggled with issues of faith and doubt. Some have been primarily activists, whose faith has been fuelled by social and pastoral action, while some have been primarily contemplatives, whose Christian witness focuses on prayer. All in all, then, no different from any other group of Christians.

But because, like it or not, bishops' spouses do often get asked to talk about themselves, about their life and their faith, many of them have been forced to think deeply about the 'winding road' of their journey with God. And to think about the way in which God does not waste provisions for the journey. Gifts given to any Christian are seldom just for their benefit, and that is particularly true for a married couple. What is given to one is given to both.

So one contributor (Sue Brookhart of Montana) writes about the gradual deepening of her faith, through prayer and study. She went to seminary in her twenties, and began her lifelong discipline of say-ing the daily offices. She submits her life regularly to examination by a spiritual director. 'I talk to God every day,' she writes. 'And once in a while, God talks to me, beyond the ordinary means of prayer and Scripture and conversations with people . . . One of those times was during my husband's election process.'

In the Episcopal Church in America, bishops are chosen through a search process that can be quite lengthy. Candidates are approached and asked to allow their names to go forward. Part way through this process, Sue's husband decided that he had mistaken God's call and should withdraw his name. But for some months Sue had been hav-ing one of those times when God talks back, and was sure that God was indeed asking her husband to be Bishop of Montana. She had not shared this knowledge with her husband because she assumed it was just something that she needed to know, in order to prepare herself for what was going to happen. But now she realized that God needed her to share it with her husband, too. What is given to one is there for both.

Several bishops' spouses study and teach theology in one way or another, independently of their spouse's calling, and although being married to a bishop has changed the way in which they have used their training, it has certainly not gone to waste. Ma Myint Myint Yee from Myanmar grew up in a village, working in the paddy fields, like all the other village children. With typical modesty, she does not talk about the work that enabled her to go and study at an Anglican Bible school and become head of the Religious Education Department in Mandalay Diocese, but she does say that she had to give it up when she got married, so as to follow her husband's calling. His training and work often kept him away from home for the first few years of their marriage, but it would not have been acceptable in their culture for her job to dictate where and how they lived. Now that her husband is a bishop, however, she finds herself in great demand as a teacher and leader, and can testify that God does not waste what he has given. 'The more I have time to serve in Mothers' Union work and to assist my husband, the more I feel that my energy to serve the Lord is increased. It is indeed the blessing of God being a bishop's wife for I have found the goodness, faithfulness and greatness of God in demanding work.'

Some bishops' spouses are themselves ordained, though there has yet to be a couple where both are bishops. As more and more Anglican provinces ordain women to the priesthood, and women and men train and work together, it is probable that there will be more ordained couples, and the Church will have to be more careful properly to deploy the gifts of both partners. At present, it can lead to problems when the bishop employs his or her own spouse, and the ordained spouse who is not the bishop can practically sink under the weight of double projections – to be both the vicar and married to the bishop is a lot to ask.

Helen van Koevering, the wife of the Bishop of Niassa in Mozambique, had just been ordained to the diaconate when her husband was asked to serve as a bishop in a diocese that did not yet have any ordained women. It was hard to see round that particular bend in God's road, when he had called both of them to ordination and then seemed to be asking Helen to submit her vocation to the Church's call to Mark to serve as a missionary bishop. While she is now a priest and able to work very fully within the diocese, she does still face some isolation and misunderstanding in a situation where the witness of their joint yet separate ministry is so very unusual. The Anglican Church is still learning how to digest it when God calls two people to be married and to be ordained. It is to be hoped that things will get easier for future Helens. But while the road has been particularly baffling, it is clear that there are real advantages to the diocese in having a bishop's wife who knows the local church so well and in having a bishop who really knows what it is like to be one of his own clergy! Helen writes: ' "God is good" and "God is great" are oft-repeated phrases in our churches, and I have learned their truth here.'

Although the problem is perhaps particularly acute for ordained spouses of bishops, it can be difficult for any spouse who works in a field that could be said to come under the bishop's jurisdiction, particularly if there is a salary involved. While many bishops' spouses do work as unpaid diocesan secretaries, administrators, co-ordinators of women's work and so on, there are generally accusations of nepotism if they are given a paid job.

Pay is not the only issue, however. One bishop's wife had to think long and hard about whether and how to continue her lay ministry as a Reader in the Church after her husband became a bishop. A Reader is called to preach and support the ordained ministry of a local church, under the direction of the vicar, so the bishop's wife had to think of how it would feel for a vicar to be in charge of the bishop's wife. Eventually, she was able to be licensed to an area team, where, she hoped, the problem would be halved by being shared.

While there are challenges for spouses who do not work in and for the Church, too, and we will look at some of those later on, the ones we have been considering have a very direct and obvious impact on how the bishop's spouse relates to God, on their spirituality, in other words. If God gives you gifts and calls you to use them and then your husband's or wife's vocation seems to make that harder, if not impossible, then there is an issue to be faced. The fact that all the contributors have faced it with courage and hope suggests something about the depth of their faith. Most of them, writing after the first challenge of their new role has passed, can see that they are further along the winding road because of what they have struggled with. Their own gifts have matured and their own contribution has become clearer, as has God's commitment to them. Not one of them felt that God had given them something and then asked them to throw it away again, even if several of them found themselves reinterpreting the shape of the original gift under the pressure of living in an episcopal household.

Every one of the contributors to this book acknowledged that being married to a bishop was a defining thing. Even if we do not think of ourselves primarily as the 'bishop's other half', we have to admit that that would be most other people's first description of us. Those who have another profession may manage to keep their secret life as a bishop's spouse from their work colleagues, but they know that in the diocese and in the local church, that's how they are known.

Some accept this way of being defined as a joy and a calling, others view it with slightly wry humour and others again are just resigned to it. Some have periods of bitter resentment about it, but bitter resentment is not a healthy state of life, and most of these bishops' spouses are eminently sensible women and men with enough grace to let go of resentment and look for the benefits, some of which we will explore later in the book.

Some of the things that bishops' spouses face are very similar to things that any clergy spouse would recognize. Judith Godfrey, who is married to the Bishop of Peru, in the Southern Cone, for example, remembers feeling quite jealous of her husband's 'commitment to God and his calling'. However much people in other professions may love their jobs, they cannot say that there is a biblical command to give them the whole of their heart, mind and soul. Yet that is what Christians are exhorted to give to our God, and many Christian couples have to look honestly at what that does to other relationships. When you add onto that the sheer relentless *busyness* of a bishop's life, it is easy to see how spouses can end up feeling that they are very much left with the dregs. Judith Godfrey found healing for her own predicament in the very God who seemed to be taking her husband away. As her own love for and knowledge of God grew, so her jealousy of her husband's calling diminished.

All the spouses who contributed to this book agreed that God and the Church cannot be just our spouse's profession. We, too, are called to be disciples and ministers of Christ, and to be members of his body, the Church. That is what keeps us going when the job seems impossible. But it does make for very mixed feelings, at times.

The Church can be a thankless employer, with poor boundaries between private and public space, vague practices about holidays and days off, laughable job descriptions and few opportunities to congratulate oneself on a job well done and completed. Yet this is the same Church in which we meet together to worship our God and whose members provide our closest community. A certain level of ambivalence about the Church is common in most clergy families, and is certainly to be found in the families of bishops, who see both the best and the worst of the wider Church. Can the Church that seems to be grinding your husband into the dust at the same time minister to the needs and hurts that it has created itself?

Again, in common with many other clergy spouses, bishops' spouses speak of a sense of isolation in the Christian community. It isn't always appropriate to share the burdens of the episcopal household with friends, and yet everyone needs to be able to share honestly. This is one of the things that a conference specifically for bishops' spouses can allow – a depth of sharing that is not always possible, except with others who know what it is like.

It is hard to imagine having a conference for doctors' spouses or lawyers' spouses, and not all bishops' spouses are comfortable with a spouses' conference. We may all be Christians and far from indifferent to what our spouses do for a living, but we are by no means unanimous in being willing to see ourselves primarily identified as 'the bishop's wife'. The issues are slightly different for 'the bishop's husband', as we shall see later on in the book. But few of that elite cohort feel that they are being primarily defined by others because of that title, in the way that many bishops' wives do.

For many of us, that is a complicated emotional and spiritual matter. As Christians we are, in theory, used to being primarily defined by our relationships, in particular, our relationship with God and our relationship with each other. The very word 'Christian' implies all of that, committing us both to Christ and to his other disciples. Many bishops' wives do, indeed, embrace their calling in that spirit. They see their husband's vocation as, inevitably, theirs, too. Many speak unaffectedly of a 'joint ministry', where the Church gets 'two for the price of one'.

But others are less confident and comfortable about such a definition. They do not feel that their Christian calling is primarily to be 'the bishop's wife', and, while they almost all support their husband's calling in a great variety of ways, as we shall see, they don't, in their heart of hearts, think of themselves as being defined by their husband's role.

We are aware that many people think we lead enviable lives, with our Christian service so clearly defined for us. We are even aware that some people think we must lead lives of impossible glamour and privilege. Some of the people who contributed to this book wondered just how much disillusionment was healthy for any readers who do not come from episcopal households, and whether it wouldn't be more edifying simply to concentrate on the power and the glory, the garden parties and the walk with God.

But the plain fact is that bishops' wives (and husbands) struggle with their sense of discipleship, just like anyone else. In a way, those who have a clear belief that they share their spouse's ministry are the lucky ones – though the actual course of their lives and the demands upon them do not grow any easier as a result of that. But while God may indeed call some couples to shared ministry, he just doesn't do so for all bishops and their spouses. Living with being defined by a title that is not chosen and doesn't seem to fit well is not easy. But in that we are no different from so many of our Christian brothers and sisters. Many people are unsure about how exactly their work and their faith fit together. Many Christians long to hear God calling them into full-time mission or ministry and instead sense that they are called to go on being Christians to the best of their ability where they are. Bishops' spouses at least know that it is unlikely that they will be able to deny their faith. They can't really pretend that their husbands are nothing to do with them! One less temptation, then, and for that we can be thankful.

Helen van Koevering
Niassa (Mozambique), married to
Rt Revd Mark van Koevering

On becoming a Christian

Being raised in the cosiness of the new town of Welwyn Garden City, England, going to Durham University in the north of England was an awakening for me. Unknown, and newly aware of both enormous privilege and great unemployment, I found myself yearning for something known in Sunday school but left behind during my teens, and unexpectedly had an experience of God's overwhelming love at a student mission in my second year. My life was turned around on that evening, and other turnings have followed: travelling after university through Asia and Australia in 1982–83, meeting Christians in mission and development work, praying for personal direction in the Australian outback, seeing God's care and concern for the poor take on personal meaning for me; leaving teaching in peaceful, rural Zimbabwe in 1989 to teach women's groups in the war-zone of central Mozambique and to work with the poorest; meeting Mark, my husband, in Maputo in 1989; going forward for ordination in 1997. To seek and walk with Jesus has been my strength, and the adventure my challenge.

Living in the shadow

We first came to Lichinga, the provincial capital of Niassa in northern Mozambique, the centre for the Diocese of Niassa, in 1991. In the 1990s, we both worked as lay community development workers, with projects happily interrupted by the coming of peace and the birth of three children. Both of us were working for the Anglican Church, Mark with development projects and I as Diocesan Secretary, before leaving for theological studies in the UK with my husband as an ordinand of Niassa. We both studied for degrees before moving to a housing-estate parish in South Wales, where I continued on a course towards ordination.

My life, with that of my family, has been completely turned around by my husband's election as Bishop of Niassa in 2003, and I have experienced much of the change as loss. Perhaps our situation is exacerbated by living within a different cultural paradigm, and much was unprecedented. I left behind the joy of my work as an ordained woman, to wait for acceptance of this by Synod in late 2004; with the poverty of education here, we let our two sons go on to boarding schools in South Africa; my husband's travels are extensive, and we are apart and/or out of communication for several months a year; and I have even lost my name, being more often called *a familia*. Some call me Vovo (Grandma) because of my husband's position, though those I work with most closely call me Mama Helena. There have been many moments of feeling either invisible in an 'other' culture – the Bishop is usually credited with or thanked for my work – or highly visible with crude sexist and racist 'street-talk'. Living in the shadow of my husband, the Bishop, is not easy.

Life in the hierarchy which is the Church here has been a tension, too, particularly to a couple committed to 'doing it differently'. This is an isolating and lonely position, little understood by family, and old, or new, friends. Niassa is a church of the poorest, working through historical neglect, war and degrading poverty. We share the illnesses of those around us, particularly malaria. When floods come or high temperatures, the effects of global climate change, we feel the effect too, with less food on the market, leaks in our house, flooding and an increase in sickness. While I enjoy the variety of people we meet, friendship is limited – I'm fluent in Portuguese, our national language, but many in our churches speak only local languages; missionaries in town have their own teams, strategies and schedules; contact with other bishops' wives is negligible; and our diocese, three times the size of the UK, is too vast to meet with the wives of our forty clergy except on flying pastoral visits. And I miss the fun of family life with our children so far away. This transition has been painful, almost too challenging, and plain hard work – with glimpses of God's smile! Like the time I understood 'sleeping on short beds', the proverbial description of an impossible situation of Isaiah 28.20, read on a visit to our Lakeshore where short, narrow, homemade beds are the norm. And like the times when visitors have understood and encouraged. It took the best part of three years to reach an equilibrium.

On being a Christian

I wear many hats in my daily life. Home-schooling my daughter fills the mornings of my week. Afternoons are varied: I sit on different diocesan committees and meetings; teach in our training weeks with community priests; support various parish links with UK churches; lead the Mothers' Union as diocesan president (and on the Provincial Executive); serve as the contact point for staff and clergy when the Bishop is travelling! For my own personal spiritual growth, I have found writing for two UK Christian publishers invaluable, though best of all is my involvement as priest of a local church. With this community of two hundred, I'm challenged by our lay-led church, the connections between traditional religion and Anglicanism, belonging and baptism, life and death, fear and love. 'God is good' and 'God is great' are oft-repeated phrases in our churches, and I have learned their truth here.

Seeing growth and change is humbling: God's strength has been proved in our weakness. Our clergy numbers have doubled to forty and our churches increased by 20 per cent; numerous development and building projects are rebuilding the Church and restoring communities; some key staff have given their skills to the people of our diocese, particularly in the area of health and HIV/AIDS; and our children are excelling in their education! I'm encouraged to believe that perhaps God has worked through our presence here. All this can only be credited to the Spirit's work – this is God's time for Mozambique, and I feel a sense of privilege about being here right now, seeing God's grace at work.

Sue Brookhart
Montana (USA), married to Rt Revd Frank Brookhart

My name is Sue Brookhart. I am the spouse of Frank Brookhart, Bishop of Montana (ECUSA). What follows are the bits of my story that address Jane's questions: how I became a Christian, the effect of Frank's election on my life, how I spend my time and how that affects my faith.

I became a Christian through infant baptism, which was more my parents' doing than mine. I grew into my own faith, and began to think about life in terms of faith. One example is a moment when I was a teenager, practising the organ in an empty church. I realized it was ironic that in that church at that time (forty years ago) I was allowed to be the organist for a church service but not to be an acolyte. I decided that it was the church's problem and not mine if they were so silly as to think it was harder to light the candles than to play the organ, and even sillier if they thought that God wanted only boys to light candles but it was all right if girls played the organ.

10

As I have grown and matured, so has my faith. The teenage example shows a one-dimensional process based solely on logic; my faith has become a more multi-dimensional process with a larger place for prayer and spiritual experience. In my early twenties, I went to seminary. I say the daily office. I have a spiritual director. So I talk to God every day. And once in a while, God talks to me, beyond the ordinary means of prayer and Scripture and conversations with people. A handful of times in my life, I have had a sure sense of something at a very deep level. One of those times was during my husband's election process.

At one point, my husband told me he thought he would withdraw from the Montana search process. I told him he might want to reconsider – that I had a strong sense he was going to be the next Bishop of Montana. In fact, I had had that message for months, but had not said anything. I thought that God had sent me that message to help me prepare for my own transition. With hindsight, of course, it makes sense that my message was also for my husband. I anticipated the transition would be difficult for me because it meant I was leaving a fulfilling position as a college professor. It would have been very easy to say I was not interested in moving anywhere that did not have a professor's position within commuting distance. I needed a message to help me disengage.

So we moved to Montana. I became an independent consultant. As I write this, I am in an airport on my way back to my university, where I still do part-time work. I also do contract work for a variety of states and schools, and I write teacher education materials. Last year, I was appointed to a term as editor of one of the academic journals in my field. It is fulfilling work, and I have ceased to worry about my professional identity. Living in Montana is a real blessing. The climate, the scenery and the people all agree with me. The view out of my window every morning inspires me to remember 'I lift up my eyes to the hills'.

I spend time in many roles: as a professional, a bishop's spouse, a community member, and homemaker and mother (less time-consuming now that our children are grown). Professionally, time depends on the week. Sometimes, like this week, I fly to some location and, except for living in a hotel room, I work fairly normal professional days for whatever client I am serving. Other times,

I work in my 'office' – a room in our house – and write on my laptop or communicate via the Internet with very flexible hours interrupted by chores or errands.

My bishop's spouse time is also varied. I have visited most of the parishes in the diocese, some several times, with my husband. Episcopal visitations in Montana, where the distances are great, are often weekend trips. When I can go, it's fun for both of us. I have attended diocesan conventions and clergy conferences.

The community part of my life is larger now than before, because of the flexibility of my work schedule. I am a member of several organizations, including the local symphony society. I am the sub-organist at the Episcopal Cathedral in Helena, and to keep up with that I have begun taking organ lessons again. This recent development has significantly decreased my parish visitations. The cathedral has just done a major addition to the organ, I love to play, and a need arose for a sub-organist. It seemed that I should use the gift I have been given in service, at least for the moment.

As to the question of how all this affects my faith, as you can see it's all a growing, almost a living, thing. I continue to pray and worship, to do my work, and to love and support my husband. What I should do is often clear, as it was when he answered the call to move to Montana. Sometimes it's not so clear. For example, a lot of sleepless nights 'wrestling with the angel' preceded the decision to give up some weekend visitations in order to do more organ playing at the cathedral.

I have always felt that both men and women need some sense of who they are in order to be whole, and even, truly, to be faithful. Thus I don't feel that God called my husband to Montana in order to end my own usefulness or service. In faith, I try to balance all my roles, including being a bishop's spouse, and trust that that will put me where God wants me to be. And when it doesn't, my past experience suggests God will tell me about it!

2

Profit and loss

———◆◆◆———

Most of the people who contributed to this book spoke about their sense of loss on moving to a bishop's job. Elizabeth San San Htay from Toungoo in Myanmar writes, 'It took years for me to stop crying after the election.' The diocese they were called to serve is particularly challenging, with significant numbers of internally displaced persons, traumatized by war and conflict. Her husband is seldom entirely safe as he travels about to visit his flock, so her reaction is understandable. Perhaps it is more extraordinary that she is also able to write, 'Finally I learned and discovered that we are called to serve the Living God who loves us so much in this particular region.'

Not many bishops' spouses have reason to feel quite such sorrow at their spouse's election to the episcopate, but very few longed for the move. That is particularly true of those who came from parish life. Liz Inwood, from Bedford, writes, 'I loved being a vicar's wife! I enjoyed the sense of teamwork, and of the vicarage being at the centre of parish life.' Her sentiments are echoed by many. She adds that it was easy to feel at home in the parish community, 'without having to earn the right to belong'.

Obviously, not all clergy families have such positive experiences of parish life, but since, on the whole, clergy are asked to be bishops because they have negotiated other parts of their ministries with success and enjoyment, the chances are that if they have been in parishes, they have done it well, with the support of their spouses and families.

Judith Nicholls, from Lancaster, remembers hitting the headlines in the press as the 'vicar's wife who danced the cancan' when she and her husband put on a fundraising concert in their parish. Although that is not a commonplace, it does express the sense of being able to use your own skills and gifts and be accepted for yourself that many people felt in parish life.

Helen Farrer, from Wangaratta in Australia, writes, 'We lived (and loved) parish life for the first thirty years of our marriage. I developed all sorts of co-ordinating, catering, care-taking, publishing and doorbell skills and felt that that was where I was meant to be and what I was meant to be doing. I was the one who could unlock the hall, provide Band-aids and safety pins, mind choirboys after practice, organize tradesmen, sit with parishioners in outpatients; all those gifts of time that give opportunities for ministry if you think about it, but you don't.' While some clergy spouses might balk at that list of things, Helen clearly flourished, and felt appreciated in parish life. She, like many others, felt like a round peg in its own perfect hole. When her husband was elected to be a bishop, she felt that 'all those years of being Martha had finished, my opportunities for ministry (as it were) were no longer there, and there was a big gap'.

Not all bishops come direct from parish life, of course. But Christine Jensen, from Sydney, still experienced something of the same sense of displacement in the move to a diocese. She and her husband had been living and working in a theological college for sixteen years before his election as a bishop. She speaks of the 'stability of that life, the rhythm of the academic year, the collegiality of the faculty', all of which she missed. 'No longer can I just walk down the street and meet the folk we're serving. . . . It's hard always meeting new people, trying to remember if you've met them before and initiating conversations all the time.'

Susan Knowles, from Sodor and Man, moved to the bishop's house from a deanery in a cathedral close. She writes that she 'belonged to the community of those living and working in and around the building [the cathedral]. I met my husband's colleagues and their wives and families frequently as we all went about our daily routines; we by no means lived in each other's pockets but our paths often crossed by chance or prior arrangement and I enjoyed the easy social contact.'

Barbara Packer, from Ripon and Leeds, also notes this change of scale, from the close relationships with relatively few people in a parish or similar community, to the more diffuse relationships with far more people in a diocese. She writes, 'I found when I moved from vicarage to bishop's house that I lost the day-by-day close relationships of the parish, which I had greatly valued. There too we practised hospitality, and many groups met in our house, with the possibility of developing relationships. Now the groups I meet are more often unknown or slightly known to me. In visiting around the diocese and attending worship too, I meet a huge number of people, often superficially. It requires a degree of extroversion that does not come naturally to me!'

Penny Brackley, from Dorking in the Diocese of Guildford, adds, 'it can feel as if one is always a visitor and not really a member of the congregation, however welcome one is made to feel'.

I certainly remember not long after my husband was elected a bishop in Wales turning up in a church rather late and very wet through from the heavy rain, having dropped my husband at the door and then gone to park the car. I told the verger who I was and I heard him turn to a colleague and say, very dubiously, 'There's a woman here who *says* she's the Bishop's wife.' It made me wonder if they got a lot of people claiming to be 'the Bishop's wife'. But it also made me feel like a not very welcome stranger.

But perhaps the problem was that I didn't fulfil the verger's expectations of what a bishop's wife ought to be like. Most clergy and their families face some stereotyping. One clergy wife tells of taking her husband, not dressed in his clerical shirt, to her work Christmas party, and discovering halfway through the evening that her colleagues were playing a game called 'Guess which one is the vicar'. She and her husband were both rather pleased that no one guessed it was him.

If all clergy are odd, bishops and their spouses are even odder, partly because, as Penny Brackley says, of 'our rarity value'. It is easier to have preconceptions undisturbed if you are not very likely to meet their subject. Most people, in Britain at least, if they have any mental picture at all of a bishop's wife, probably think of a Mrs Proudie figure. Anthony Trollope described Mrs Proudie as the bishop in all but name, a meddling, bigoted, powerful woman, always sure that she knew best.

In fact, of course, bishops and their spouses are as diverse as any other group of professionals. And while bishops may have a certain amount of professional expertise, training and experience in common, their spouses are likely to be even more different from one another. As Celia McCulloch, from Manchester, says, 'people seem to think that from the moment of your husband's consecration you yourself have, by some process of osmosis, become an expert in theology, hotel management, being a company director, and full of confidence!' But, as Kathy Gregg, from Eastern Oregon, says, 'there is no manual for the spouse of a bishop'. Even in the provinces that do have some practical written guidance that gets passed to new bishops' spouses, that advice cannot tell you how to *be*, or suddenly enable you to change the person you are, even if you wanted to.

Since most, if not all, bishops' spouses would like to support the ministry of the bishop as well as they can, they do try to find out what is expected of them. But that can be hard. Most people have grandiose but vague ideas of what a bishop's spouse should be like and should do.

In some parts of the Anglican Church worldwide, those expectations can be very high indeed. Louise Morais-Neufville, from Liberia, writes, 'there is a tendency on the part of the people not to allow you to be yourself. Their expectations are so high that to express your anger, displeasure or emotions is far below their expectation. The Bishop's wife is to remain calm and serene at all times. Even if she is hurting, people will raise an eyebrow if it is the reverse.' Since Louise's husband was a bishop in Liberia during a time of brutal and bloody war, it was indeed a bit much if her congregations expected her to remain calm at all times.

Louise is not alone in feeling rather lonely under the weight of expectation. Most bishops' wives in Africa are called 'Mama', and are expected to be just that towards their husband's flock. They are expected to be the heart of the diocese, warm and comforting and always ready to meet the needs of others. Many of them spoke of feeling themselves to be under scrutiny, with faintly hostile eyes waiting for them to put a foot wrong. A spouse's behaviour, if less than perfect, can provide another stick with which to beat the Bishop.

Not all bishops' spouses carry quite such a burden of expectation, but many do feel that, even if people cannot really tell you what a bishop's wife ought to be like, they know when you've got it wrong. Denise Inge, from Worcester, writes, 'I keep forgetting I *am* the wife of a bishop – that there are things, like names, I *ought* to know, things I ought to *do* and ought *not* to do. Like popping out quickly to the shops on your bike in your shorts on a hot summer day.'

Hilary Hill, from Guildford, was aware one Sunday, of being under quite close scrutiny from a woman in church who finally leaned over and said, 'I know who you are, you're the lady that buys all that cheese.' Hilary adds, 'She worked on the delicatessen counter in the local Tesco [supermarket] where I would stock up on large quantities of cheese when we were entertaining clergy. The next thing she said was, "You're really quite normal, you're just like us!" What was she expecting?' Hilary asks herself. 'What do people expect? A large badge saying "Bishop's wife" – a bit like "Beware of the dog"? Some kind of identity mark?'

Not being quite sure what it is that people expect of us is part of the problem, and whatever it is, most of us know we are not it. The great majority of people are delighted to have their unformu-lated preconceptions overturned, and to discover that the bishop's spouse is 'just like us'. But some are disappointed. After I had been speaking at a meeting, a kind friend relayed that people had been saddened by my informality. They felt that they had not quite got what they came for.

But if some of us are uncomfortable and some positively weighed down by the weight of expectation of a bishop's spouse, all are also aware of the enormous privileges offered to us because we are mar-ried to a bishop. The one most often mentioned by those who wrote for this book was the sheer pleasure of access to such a variety of people. Bishops go into schools, prisons, shops and palaces, as well as all kinds of churches, as a welcome guest, and their spouses often go with them. Lorene Noble, from North Queensland, says, 'I have driven thousands of kilometres and sometimes lived in homes that were totally unsuitable for the ministry we were in and where little support was available. However, they have also brought contact with a wide variety of people and many shared experiences that I believe are unique to the work my husband is involved in. The need to encourage people in their Christian walk is ever present and espe-cially needed where people are isolated or experiencing demanding working and living conditions.'

Many – though not all – bishops' spouses are involved in the care and nurture of other clergy spouses and families. Marsha Klusmeyer, from West Virginia, writes, 'Another interest my husband and I have had since coming to West Virginia is clergy spouses and families, and how the diocese can be supportive of them. We've had several retreats, set up an email network, have a monthly prayer chain and get spouses together at our diocesan convention, usually for lunch and an outing.'

Christine Jensen, from Sydney, writes, 'I do have a deep concern for the spouses of those serving in ministry in our churches both lay and ordained. Life is often a struggle and people work very hard. They are in the frontline of ministry and need every encouragement and support.'

The size of the diocese and the resources available to it inevitably affect the way in which the bishop's spouse will be involved in care of clergy families. A bishop's wife in Kenya told me that most confirmation services involve a trip of several days, taking everything you might need for the journey with you, including fuel, food and spare parts for the van. It might not be quite like that in Montana, but Sue Brookhart, too, writes, 'Episcopal visitations in Montana, where the distances are great, are often weekend trips.'

Comfort Fearon, from Nigeria, has very few clergy families under her care. When her husband arrived in his newly created missionary diocese there were only three priests in what was a predominantly Muslim area. But the poverty of the diocese meant that Comfort had to take her 'maternal' role in relation to its people very seriously indeed. Since her husband is also an archbishop, she has the care of several bishops' wives and families.

As Nara Duncan, from Pittsburgh, writes, 'a bishop's wife can do a lot of leading'. She adds, 'I have discovered that a bishop's spouse has a "bully pulpit". That is, people have to listen to us because of who we are – and because most people are polite.' While such a privilege has to be exercised with caution, Nara writes, 'We get to take people to places they might never go. I was able to tell our diocesan family about an orphanage in Rwanda that needed building, a hospital that was destroyed during the genocide that needed fixing. I get to take groups of clergy wives to Uganda to see for themselves what kinds of difference they can make . . . I know that I can only reach a few people, but because I am a bishop's spouse, those few are more than if I were not.'

Like Nara, many spouses write about the joys of being part of a worldwide Church. Every diocese in the Anglican Communion has a complex set of formal and informal relationships with other churches and dioceses around the world. Bishops and their families will number among their close friends people from all around the world, and will be able to pray in an informed way about situations that most people only read about in the newspapers. It may not be the privilege that most people would associate with episcopal ministry, but it comes very high on the list for many bishops and their spouses.

In some parts of the Church, this is particularly apparent. Judith Godfrey, for example, serves with her husband in South America. They thought they were going as missionaries for six years, but found that God had other ideas. When her husband was made the first Bishop of Uruguay, she writes, 'Our brief now was to start a new diocese from scratch with no financial resources, no training, and, interestingly (!), no clergy. We found a team of missionary priests and their families to come and help us start parishes and projects . . . We had people from the UK, USA, Canada, Australia, New Zealand, Colombia and Uruguay all trying to settle in and minister together . . . We all had to learn some new skills, and pray hard for tolerance and love!'

Judith's experience of living in a world Church may have been particularly vivid, but that sense of being part of a very big family, of all races, cultures and classes is part of being married to an Anglican bishop. It is something that the Lambeth Conference brings centre stage, but that remains a part of the work of a bishop throughout his or her ministry.

In many parts of the world, bishops and their families do not only mix with other Christians. Increasingly, leaders of all religions have to forge relationships for the benefit of the whole community that they serve together. In areas where Christians are very much in a minority, that can be hard, as we shall see in another chapter. But in some countries, bishops' spouses identify this as another part of the rich variety that being married to a bishop brings. Linda Baines, from Croydon, writing about a 'typical' week in her life, says, 'The local imam and his family came for lunch on Sunday. He and Nick [Linda's husband] are planning to be in debate at an event in Croydon soon and often meet at civic functions.'

Although all the people who wrote for this book were honest about the challenges of being married to a bishop, every single contribution mentioned the privilege, too. Most particularly they were grateful to God's people, who pray for and love their bishops and families. Above all, they were grateful to God for entrusting them with such varied, exciting and humbling lives.

Susan Knowles
Sodor and Man (Isle of Man; now St Paul's Cathedral, London), married to Rt Revd Graeme Knowles

When it was announced that my husband was to be the next Bishop of Sodor and Man, he was Dean of Carlisle and we lived in the cathedral close. I worshipped at the cathedral regularly on Sundays and sometimes on weekdays and belonged to the community of those living and working in and around the building. I met my husband's colleagues and their wives and families frequently as we all went about our daily routines; we by no means lived in each other's pockets but our paths often crossed by chance or prior arrangement and I enjoyed the easy social contact. I had had a career as an English teacher for thirty years and then in Carlisle had done more-or-less full-time supply work at a city comprehensive. We had been there for five years and there was a comfortable familiarity about it all. The move to the Isle of Man would involve some significant changes!

The first of these became apparent on the day my husband's appointment was announced – at a press conference, which was a new experience for me. Because both Carlisle and the Isle of Man fall within the area covered by ITV Border, there were television reporters and cameras present as well as representatives from the newspapers and Manx Radio. I hadn't been prepared for the event to have such a high profile. The Bishop has a significant role in the political life of the island, so on that initial visit we were also presented to the President of Tynwald, the Chief Minister and the First Deemster (the senior judge), and, as I followed in my husband's wake, I began to realize that I was now the consort of a Public Figure! This impression was confirmed when we moved to the island and I was visited by the social correspondent of the newspaper who – extraordinarily – wanted to write an article about me and include a photograph. I was sorry that my parents were no longer alive to see me featuring in a gossip column! Other articles and photographs have followed and this means that I am often recognized in the street and in shops, and people greet me, even if they do not actually know me. This was unnerving at first but the population of the Isle of Man is under 80,000 and there is a strong sense of community, so such open friendliness is not unusual. My husband has to be away quite often and it is reassuring to know that I can comfortably go to social and cultural events on my own, confident that there will be people there whom I know. Equally, we can never go anywhere on the island without being seen – and without our presence there being referred to later by someone else!

I have always been a committed churchgoer and it was important for me to establish quickly what my pattern would be. Many people expected me to accompany my husband wherever he went on a Sunday but I knew that I needed to belong to a church family and play a part in its life, so I worship at our local parish church. There, though clearly not anonymous, I am accepted as an ordinary member of the congregation and I contribute to activities whenever I can, enjoying keenly the friendship and fellowship of that community. Often, though, I am absent at key times of the year when I go with my husband to special services elsewhere, and I am conscious of the occasional haphazardness of my attendance – just as I am conscious of the fact that I no longer enjoy regular public worship in the same place as my husband, something which for many years I took for granted.

Although I settled quickly and happily, for the first twelve months I found it difficult to adapt to a life without a fixed routine. For many people the fact that every day is different is a delight: for me it is a nightmare! After a lifetime organized around the ringing of school bells, I now had to manage my own time – in a new country and a new role, with no ready-made tasks to complete. I learned quickly that the gaps in my days could be filled many times over, and with a longstanding commitment to the Protestant work ethic I was soon back in the state of chasing my tail and having to take care not to double-book the diary. I was invited to join committees, both social and charitable, and became particularly involved with the Isle of Man Adoption Service (which is a church organization) and with Victim Support (which is not). I am also a school governor and give literacy support at the same school. All of these roles were offered to me because I am the Bishop's wife but in almost every case consideration had been given to what was known of my past experience and my skills. I have also opened innumerable fêtes and fairs, set off balloons at the start of a United Nations Association sixth-form debate, presented the prizes at an Essentially Dancing contest and judged a bonny babies competition. There is no lack of variety in the things I am called upon to do!

I was also asked by some of the clergy wives (and it was the wives, though one husband sometimes joins us) if we could arrange to meet on a regular basis. Sometimes, I think, a bishop and/or his wife can feel isolated, especially after living and working as part of a team, and the developing of friendships with clergy families has been a joy. Ambitiously, we spouses meet monthly and plan a varied programme. These gatherings are a significant part of my social life – and a source of much good fun.

The most surprising thing that has happened has been the number of requests that I receive to speak to groups, mostly of women but sometimes mixed and very occasionally of men. They wanted to hear about my life as a bishop's wife and, foolishly, I accepted the first invitation soon after our arrival, quickly realizing that I knew nothing yet of the subject on which I was to speak. As the months passed, I gradually became aware that the same faces were beginning to appear in different groups – always a problem on a small island – and that the stories were starting to sound a bit stale as the novelty wore off. Since then I have reverted to my roots as an English teacher and now take a light-hearted approach to some literary topics, such as 'Clergy Wives in Books' and 'Desert Island Books'. I still find speaking nerve-racking, but the groups are usually small and – once again – people are immensely friendly and appreciative. I did wonder, however, just what I was doing when I responded to a message on the answerphone and was asked if I was 'the lady who does talks about living with the Bishop'!

Is this what I am reduced to – a channel of information about the inner workings of the Bishop's household? I hope not! I support my husband's ministry in conventional ways through hospitality and by attending public functions, and I do so willingly, but the uniqueness of the Diocese of Sodor and Man has probably given me more opportunity than most bishops' wives to pursue avenues that interest and challenge me within the broad remit of the role of the Bishop's wife.

Liz Inwood
Bedford (St Albans Diocese, England), married to Rt Revd Richard Inwood

I loved being a vicar's wife! I enjoyed the sense of teamwork, and of the vicarage being at the centre of parish life. I appreciated people's expectation that I would willingly share their joys and their tales of woe, their triumphs and their failures. I was 'just' one of them and somehow belonged, without having to earn the right to belong. It was fun, as a family, to worship together, and participate together in the events that take place in a lively parish. It was easy to feel that we were working together, and had complementary ministries – even the children, as they brought friends along to the youth work.

When my husband became an archdeacon, there was a real sense of bereavement, as that way of life disappeared. There's always a great feeling of loss in leaving a parish, and leaving behind all the folk with whom you've shared so much, and indeed in any move, as you lose your network of friends and acquaintances, work colleagues, and even the doctor, dentist, hairdresser and local shops! But this time my whole role disappeared. Archdeacons visit the clergy and wardens; it's less often the other way round. Phone calls are very much business and I wasn't expected to be involved, generally speaking. I lost count of the times I was told, 'I was hoping to get the answerphone.' They meant, 'I didn't mean to disturb you', but it wasn't very affirming! I did enjoy the call from a young clergy wife who was very relieved to find that her husband's new mystery BT 'best friend' was only the archdeacon!

The family and I made our home in a local parish, which was great, though we missed sharing worship with Dad. His 'events' and ours were different, and we had to learn new ways of sharing. I did get to know many of the clergy through inviting them to suppers in our home, and participating in their parish events with my husband when I was invited to do so. The diocesan senior staff and their spouses were a new source of friendship and support, though at a distance. I built up new work opportunities and networks, as one does . . . and then my husband became a bishop.

At least I'd already learned how not to be a vicar's wife. The move was exciting, with the thrill of the consecration, and the daunting sense of new expectations. For him a whole new set of unfamiliar clothes and an enormous number of new challenges; for me the prospect of working out where I fitted into it all.

The family were no longer at home. Would I go with him to the services he was taking, or have a church base of my own? Would I look for a permanent job, or something more flexible that would leave me available to share in some of the interesting occasions we were invited to be part of? I compromised. It was fun to travel with him, and to get to know the area and the parishes, and take part in a rich variety of worship experiences. People were very welcoming, though not always quite sure what to do with a bishop's wife, who arrived very early and stayed very late (and was actually quite happy to be ignored). But it did mean there was no continuity of fellowship, and sometimes, dare I say it, a repeat sermon. So increasingly I go to a local parish church, who have kindly accepted me, and where I have made friends and feel like one of the family.

Opting for a more flexible style of work does mean being able to take advantage of some fascinating opportunities, which are certainly varied – from meeting royalty to washing up in a wonderfully multicultural parish hall, and from leading pilgrimages abroad to watching sods cut as a redundant church is adapted for a youth centre. It's a privilege being involved in a great variety of special celebrations, both locally and across the country.

Entertaining in our home is the most obvious way in which we can operate as a team, and we enjoy having people here. Sometimes it's possible to be involved with clergy families, though I certainly wouldn't want to interfere where that's not welcomed. And, like any other Christian, I can find areas of service and ministry that are suited to my gifts.

The answer to the question that I get asked, 'What's it like being married to a bishop?' is always, 'I like being married to my bishop!'

Helen Farrer
Wangaratta (Australia), married to Rt Revd David Farrer

After a very ordinary C. of E. upbringing (sent to Sunday school, confirmed at 14, regarded confirmation as the Church's Leaving Certificate), at the age of 17 I began to train as a nurse. It was then that I first saw the effect of illness, old age and approaching death upon people and their families.

Something in me realized that there was a dimension to life that I lacked, that was important to me both as a person and as a nurse. One Sunday evening I crept into the back of the church nearest the hospital (it happened to be Melbourne's High Church) and was immediately caught up in an amazing, totally unfamiliar, world of mystery and spirituality.

After some months I braved the morning service and then weekday festival days: gradually I became part of the parish. My husband-to-be was a parishioner there, although I didn't focus on him for nearly three years!

We lived (and loved) parish life for the first thirty years of our marriage. I developed all sorts of co-ordinating, catering, care-taking, publishing and doorbell skills and felt that that was where I was meant to be and what I was meant to be doing. I was the one who could unlock the hall, provide Band-aids and safety pins, mind choirboys after practice, organize tradesmen, sit with parishioners in outpatients; all those gifts of time that give opportunities for ministry if you think about it, but you don't. During those years I also worked as a labour-ward midwife, taught nurses and wrote textbooks. Our two sons seemed to enjoy their childhood involved with it all.

Then David was elected to a country diocese. It was too far from my former work for me to continue and the few shifts that I worked in the local midwifery unit showed me that the staff were uncom-fortable working with The Bishop's Wife. Also, we live in a large and beautiful house and the church and community expectations were that the Bishop's wife should be At Home when she was not at meet-ings or mission committees.

Life was suddenly very different. After about a year it hit me that all those years of being Martha had finished, my opportunities for ministry (as it were) were no longer there, and there was a big gap. I went with David on all his visits to parishes and had some very varied liturgical experiences. But I felt that it was my body and not much more of me at church. I missed the rhythm of the Church's year: it got lost in confirmations, dedications, centenaries and inductions. I wasn't very good at singing the Lord's song in such a strange land. I got to know our clergy but felt it inappropriate to burden them with me because of their relationship with my husband.

A priest friend from years ago helped me to start again with some long discussions, a return to confession and a lot of telephone support for a year or two. Now I see a local Roman Catholic priest who helps me to think through my faith and prayer life and that helps keep things in perspective. When I asked him what I should read to help my faith he said, 'Um . . . the Bible?'

Nine years on, this is what I do for the Church: most of the work involved in publishing our diocesan newspaper, maintaining our diocesan website, being secretary of the diocesan branch of Anglican Missions, catering for occasional big diocesan events and the monthly Bishop-in-Council dinners and quite a lot of smaller meetings over lunch, having fairly frequent overnight visitors, opening the house to community groups and neighbouring schools for events, hauling hoses around the church properties because no one else lives close enough to water them at night. Perhaps there is more.

What I do for me is bell-ringing, which I started three years ago, and so now go on Sunday visits to parishes only every second week. This makes my bishop unhappy half of the time and the tower captain unhappy for the other half of the time. My bell-ringing friends are a precious group who have nothing to do with my husband's work (although some go to church).

Daily Bible readings and reflection provide the base for a prayer time that sometimes feels as though it is going well. Without it I know that I would be lonely even though life is full of people. I know that my faith has given me strength to encourage others and I pray that that will continue. My most important ministry is to look after my David so that he can look after his people: encouragement forms a big part of that care for him.

3

Home and family

Bishops' homes come in all shapes and sizes. Not all bishops live in palaces. In fact, very few of them do. One bishop's wife who has had to move quite regularly because of her husband's ministry says, with a laugh, that she could do with 'standard window sizes across the country'. There is a limit to how many times you can reshape a pair of curtains!

Nearly all bishops' spouses, including the ones who have employment outside the home, see hospitality as central to the ministry of a bishop, and nearly all of them are involved in providing that hospitality, though some have more help with that than others. Wendy Pritchard, from Oxford, sees hospitality to clergy as 'a way of affirming them and showing them that they matter to us. Many have very difficult working situations, and deserve much recognition and encouragement.'

Judith Nicholls, from Sheffield, makes the most of the large house and garden that go with her husband's job: 'I cook for innumerable dinner parties and receptions for up to a hundred and twenty people and open up the house and garden for the use of handicapped people and various charities. I suppose I must have raised something in the region of £100,000 over the past ten years . . . Disabled adults and children love coming to Bishopscroft and enjoyed our delightful garden during the summer months . . . The number of visitors to the house must amount to several thousand each year.'

Celia McCulloch, from Manchester, writes: 'Hospitality and spirituality, based on the hospitality of Abraham (Genesis 18), have always been part of who I am. Therefore it was natural for me to exercise them in supporting my husband in his work. This primarily involved opening our home to all comers, cooking and serving countless meals, from one or two people to more than a hundred.

If the numbers were over a hundred and fifty I would enlist the help of caterers. I regarded such hospitality as part of my gift to make every person feel they were valued.'

If you stop and think how much time is involved in catering for a large group of people, from shopping, to cooking, to serving, to clearing up, this is a significant gift of time and love that bishops' spouses offer to the Christian community. It says something vital about the ministry of a bishop. A bishop is not just an executive or a manager, or even a teacher and a spiritual leader. A bishop is also someone who helps to draw the Church together. So a bishop's home is saying something profound about the nature of the relationship between the bishop and the people. A bishop's home is the 'family' home, where all the children, even after they've grown up, know they will be welcomed and fed. Most of the spouses who contributed to this book know that instinctively, and love this part of the role.

But, with the best will in the world, a profound theology of hospitality cannot always provide the material resources necessary. A number of bishops' wives, particularly from Asia and Africa, are honest enough to admit that there are times when it is impossible to make the food go round. Before any large service or diocesan occasion, people expect to gather in considerable numbers in the bishop's grounds and be fed and cared for. Catherine Brient, from Sunyani in Ghana, writes about 'the pressure that is brought to bear on the personal finances of the Bishop's wife because of a desire to receive every Tom, Dick and Harry who visits with a befitting refreshment'.

Nor is it even just the occasional meal, after which people will go home. In many parts of the world, local Christians expect to be able to use their bishop's house as a hostel, if they need to. Ma Myint Myint Yee, from Myanmar, writes: 'Our house was always filled with visitors from the villages who came to town for various purposes, church members and students. So I had to serve them.' One bishop's wife from Sudan has had a man living with them for three years, eating at the family's expense. But the tradition of hospitality and the Bishop's duty of care mean that they just have to put up with it.

There can be an assumption that bishops are rich as well as loving and pastoral. Many bishops' spouses have faced real indignation when unable to give all the material help a needy Christian might demand. Bishops' houses can add to that misconception, because they do tend to be larger than the homes of most of their clergy and parishioners. But bishops' salaries do have to stretch a long way if the whole diocese feels that they have a claim on the bishop and his family.

Although very few bishops' spouses in Britain and America have such extreme demands made upon them, I think we would all recognize that sense that a bishop's home is never just a private place. Most of the time, we accept that with grace and even enjoyment, but it is something that raises tensions for even the most committed of bishops' spouses.

The tensions can be quite minor. Rebecca Cottrell, from Reading, admits to having to clean up more frequently and thoroughly than she might if her home wasn't open to so many visitors. She describes, as part of her typical day, shopping for lunch things for visitors and making 'a bigger effort of tidying the kitchen as it is there they will be eating. Even though I don't mind eating in a bit of a mess I didn't want a complete stranger doing the same. By just before 10 o'clock I have thoroughly spring-cleaned the kitchen and downstairs toilet. (Having three boys it is sometimes a half-hour mop-out in there.)'

Housework has never been very high on my list of priorities, either. Some people are kind enough to say that it is nice to feel they are coming into a real home. Others just look shocked. We have tended to try and keep one child-free room into which unexpected visitors can be ushered without bringing a blush to my cheek. But it doesn't always work, and, like Rebecca, I find it is usually the bathroom that lets me down!

Many bishops' spouses also have the interesting and occasionally challenging task of sharing their home with people who think of it as essentially an office or workplace. Most bishops have at least a secretary, and sometimes a whole staff, who work in the bishop's home. It is understandable that they don't always remember that, to the bishop's spouse and children, it is still their home, even during office hours. Quite a few bishops' wives have been made to feel rather in the way. It is one of the many anomalies of 'working over the shop'. While many spouses value the company of the staff, particularly when the bishop is away, many are also honest enough to admit that there can be rivalry between a secretary and a spouse. Whose job is it to welcome visitors to the bishop's office and to take morning coffee to a meeting? In a parish, there would be no one else to do that, so many spouses have been in the habit of being the doorkeeper, phone answering machine and coffee-maker for years, and cannot immediately unlearn those habits when moving to a bishop's house. One bishop's wife says that being married to a bishop is a bit like being in a polygamous marriage. 'This is because . . . a bishop virtually signs a marriage contract with the Church which he oversees. Thus the bishop thence has two "wives". His heart and mind, as well as his time and financial resources, are shared between his first wife and his second "wife" (his diocese).'

But while many bishops' spouses have never experienced any problems like that, and the ones who have are usually able to smile, if wryly, about it, it is different when the public nature of the bishop's home impinges on the children. Catherine Brient, from Ghana, writes of the challenge of 'having to handle children in the family single-handedly, often because the father or grandfather is often away on a trek or is in one meeting or another, even when he is at home'. Ma Myint Myint Yee, from Myanmar, describes the sheer exhaustion of looking after her three sons as well as providing endless meals and beds for visitors. 'These made me very tired,' she admits.

Most clergy with school-age children have to struggle to find family time. Weekends, Christmas, Easter – all the times the children have free – are among the busiest times for clergy. Denise Inge, from Worcester, describes Christmas morning in a way that most bishops with children would recognize: 'the children pounce on the bed and you all open stockings and then, instead of descending upon the parcels waiting round the tree below, he puts on the uniform, untangles himself from the clinging arms of children and off he goes to a prison full of sex offenders where neither you nor the girls can follow. You know that this, though it flies in the face of every other family's routine across the country, though it leaves you lonely and hassled (of all days Christmas), your children frustrated, everyone halted in the midst of celebration and the fizz of excitement spoiling, is what he was born for and what, deep down, you believe in.'

How many Saturdays a month is it reasonable to tell your children they can't have friends round because the house will be full of visitors? Particularly if your house is the one that all the friends most want to come to, because of the space and the garden? How many of us have had to warn teenage children about appropriate clothing for sunbathing in the garden, in deference to visitors' pacemakers? How do you choose between your son's school open evening and the large diocesan party that you are supposed to be hosting, and that was in the diary a year ago, long before you had your son's school timetable?

But if the day-to-day pressures of time and of the use of the home are hard, it is even harder when children get caught in the spotlight because of what their father does. More than one adult child of a bishop has had to face unfair media attention on their divorce or their driving offence, because of having a parent who is the bishop. The relish with which people discuss things that would, in most families, be private can be very hurtful.

Most bishops' spouses feel that the positives outweigh the negatives for themselves and their families. But it is sometimes a pretty close-run thing. At the spouses' conference of Lambeth 2008, bringing up Christian families is one of the topics we shall be looking at. I hope we will be honest enough to acknowledge that our being married to a bishop doesn't automatically make our children long to go to church! If we sometimes feel that the Church is our spouse's 'other woman', our children, too, sometimes feel that everyone experiences the bishop's parental care except the bishop's own children. We know that, in theory, we and our children will be the richer for sharing with others the privileges that God has given us, but bringing theory and practice together can sometimes be a real challenge.

Celia McCulloch
Manchester (England), married to
Rt Revd Nigel McCulloch

Over the twenty-one years that I have been a bishop's wife I have noticed changing emphases on how I have related to my husband's episcopal ministry. These changes are no doubt the result of a number of factors: the needs of our children as they grew from being only 8 and 10 through adolescence to leaving home; the changing patterns of clergy wives in paid employment (and therefore the consequent changing expectations for clergy wives' support); the advent of male spouses; my own growing up from a 31-year-old new bishop's wife to my 50s; and the differing traditions and expectations from three very different dioceses where he has been a bishop – one rural, one mining/textile, and one multi-ethnic/multi-faith/cosmopolitan/commercial.

Hospitality and spirituality, based on the hospitality of Abraham (Genesis 18), have always been part of who I am. Therefore it was natural for me to exercise them in supporting my husband in his work. This primarily involved opening our home to all comers, cooking and serving countless meals, from one or two people to more than a hundred. If the numbers were over a hundred and fifty I would enlist the help of caterers. I regarded such hospitality as part of my gift to make every person feel they were valued.

Having the privilege of living in a large house with acres of ground, in one place I created a prayer garden for the diocese. I provided prayer materials and the place became a quiet sacred space available for use six days a week for parishes to retreat to in the midst of an urban diocese.

It is a great privilege being married to a bishop, and while acknowledging that I am 'the Bishop's wife' and that is how people see me, I have resisted conforming to expectations and traditions (because trying to be something I am not would destroy the uniqueness of the person God made, and the person my husband fell in love with), so I have never tried to be anything other than myself. But, although there have been times when things have not been easy, and times of pain, on the whole I have been lucky because I have always felt called to be, in my own way, a 'traditional' clergy wife.

Being a bishop's wife means that many people seem to think that from the moment of your husband's consecration you yourself have, by some process of osmosis, become an expert in theology, hotel management, being a company director, and full of confidence! In England a few bishops' wives do now have full-time careers, and many are in part-time work, but there is still an unspoken expectation that they will accompany their husbands, if not to parish services and other parish events, then at least to the 'grand' church occasions, national and civic events.

Home and family

Strangely enough, by the grace of God, I have found I can stretch myself to do more than I imagined, but I have also learned that I am not an expert in everything and now have the courage to say no when I wish to. Over the years the things I have found myself doing range through the likes of leading Bible studies, organizing and leading quiet days, arranging varied programmes for clergy spouses, feeding people, running a big house and garden, taking some of the responsibility for the care of clergy spouses and their families, doing a stint as Mothers' Union diocesan president, arranging spiritual accompaniment training for the diocese, being a member of the Church of England Mission, Evangelism and Renewal Committee, speaking at an Anglican Communion conference in the USA, representing bishops' wives on a Church Commissioners' committee, and so on. I was able to do such things because I chose, when our children were born, to give up my full-time work – buying and selling racehorses – in order to raise the children and support my husband.

Being a bishop's wife also opens doors to meet people, experience diversity of faiths and cultures and travel in a way no tourist can. I have led parties to the Holy Land and Taizé, travelled to various dioceses in places like Zambia, Tanzania, Botswana, Australia, once going on my own to Tanzania for a month at the invitation of the local bishop to engage with his diocese on women's issues.

Now my experience of being a bishop's wife is changing again, and my husband and I are working out how I can continue to enable our home to be a place of welcome and hospitality, and support him in the wide variety of ways I have done in the past, while I myself am physically less involved. These changes are happening because I am in training for full-time stipendiary parish ministry. I have felt such a call since I was 16, and have always sensed that my ministry was complementary to my husband's, not an add-on extra to his.

As a bishop's wife I have experienced both loneliness and fellowship, pressures of expectations but also wonderful support. But I don't believe these are issues related only to bishops' wives. Therefore, whether a bishop's wife or not, it is important that people are able to find support networks, whether in their families, with friends, or in other ways that suit them personally.

I hope that bishops' wives the world over are able to celebrate who they are as individuals, uniquely created in God's image and released to respond in whatever way they feel is right. I pray that the Church will be supportive by allowing each to develop and grow, whether as a traditional hands-on bishop's wife, or in secular work, full-time ministry or any other way that allows them to live life 'abundantly'.

Catherine Brient
Sunyani (Ghana), married to
Rt Revd Thomas Ampah Brient

The falling of the mantle

Very few women (if any) started as a bishop's wife. The trend has been: you get married to a man, he gets called into the priesthood, making you become a priest's wife; then if God so pleases, he gets called to become a bishop, automatically converting you into a bishop's wife.

The office of the bishop, beyond being a highly spiritual calling, is also a high public office. His counterpart in secular administration is the regional minister or at least a metropolitan chief executive. As the wife of the man occupying such an office, the title of Mother Superior catches up with you before you realize it and suddenly imposes upon you a myriad of challenges which you can learn to handle only while on the job. In a way it is like Elijah casting his mantle upon Elisha and Elisha having to follow without an option, only to learn on the job.

A 'polygamous marriage' – the source of great challenges

The challenges of being a bishop's wife are in some ways similar to the challenges faced by a wife in a polygamous marriage. This is because the priest, upon becoming a bishop, virtually signs a marriage contract with the Church which he oversees. Thus the bishop has two 'wives'. His heart and mind, as well as his time and financial resources, are shared between his first wife and his second 'wife' (his diocese). Indeed, his physical presence is also shared between his 'wives'. It appears that this 'heaven-approved

34

polygamous marriage' is the basis of most of the challenges faced by the wife of the bishop. The challenges exist while the man is a priest but they assume an exceptionally heightened dimension when the priest begins to wear a mitre and carries the crosier.

The Bishop's wife's dilemma in prayer

A wife rejoices and glories in the progress and promotion of her husband. A wife therefore carries a prayer burden on her heart for her husband in this direction. However, the progress and prosperity of the Bishop's work means increased devotion to his God and the service of his diocese. To say his availability to his marital home does not suffer loss will be playing the ostrich. It appears that the progress of the Bishop's ministry means reduced availability to his family. The dilemma for the Bishop's wife therefore is: should I continue to pray for the growth and prosperity of this man's ministry, seeing that the growth means increasing responsibility for my husband and, following in the wake of that development, increasing unavailability in the marital home? Challenging though it is, we are yet to hear of a bishop's wife trying to wrestle her husband away from a busy schedule so as to have more of him for herself!

Bits and pieces of the challenge

To cut the story short it may be appropriate to itemize some of the challenges, since they cannot all be discussed in detail:

- The unavailability of your husband due to a busy schedule and numerous travels.
- Deprivation of privacy because of numerous visitors streaming to the Bishop's court almost all day long.
- The challenge of hosting visitors with widely varying backgrounds, sometimes at very short notice.
- The pressure that is brought to bear on the personal finances of the Bishop's wife because of a desire to receive every Tom, Dick and Harry who visits with a befitting refreshment.
- The challenge of playing mother to all the clergymen and their wives, not to mention the members of the cathedral in the case where the Bishop's court is on the same premises as the cathedral – there is the general feeling within the diocese that the

Bishop's wife is a super-human mother – cannot be offended, cannot ever run short of food and can't ever run out of finances and can entertain visitors twenty-four hours a day, each day of the year.

- The challenge of having to handle children in the family single-handedly, often because the father or grandfather is often away on a trek or is in one meeting or another, even when he is at home.
- Enduring the criticisms from various quarters in the diocese about your husband the Diocesan when there is a crisis in the Church and things are not running smoothly, especially when rumours are rife that the Bishop has been involved in financial scandals.
- The challenge of dealing with difficulties and disagreements between you and the Bishop as your husband in view of his special spirituality.
- The challenge of having to appear with the Bishop publicly as Mother Superior at times and on occasions in which you have little interest and are ill-prepared, especially when the occasion demands that Mother Superior should say a word or two.
- Etc.

A tiny but important respite

Romans 8.37 says, 'Yet in all these things we are more than conquerors through him who loved us' (NKJV).

After outlining these challenges it would be unfair not to mention the moments of respite that make it all worthwhile. One of such periods is the time spent travelling together. We often have important discussions during this period, especially if the journey lasts a few hours. Another such period is the time spent having devotions together. These are times when burdens are brought to the cross and shared together. The strength received from these short devotions seems to equip the Bishop's wife with a fortitude I am still yet to understand.

The challenges of being a bishop's wife may be numerous, but the grace received for sharing in the ministry of the Bishop as his wife seems to be more than sufficient for the challenge. To God be all the glory. Amen!

God bless you.

4

'Bishop's wife but still myself'

———◆◆◆———

That is, in fact, the title of a book written some years ago. It says a great deal in a very few words. The 'but' is particularly instructive, because it does suggest that being 'myself' is a bit of a struggle against expectations, both those of others and, sometimes, one's own.

Most of the people who contributed to this book would recognize the struggle, to a greater or lesser extent, but perhaps the picture changes somewhat when being a bishop's spouse is not a full-time job. A great many bishops' spouses now have employment of their own, either paid or unpaid, and while that complicates things in some ways, it also makes retaining a sense of individual identity much easier.

Most of the spouses who work are aware that it makes life uncomfortably busy. Rebecca Cottrell, from Reading in England, writes of a day which veers wildly from catering for a meeting in the Bishop's house, to getting the children ready for school, to writing lesson plans and end-of-term reports. 'By the time I get to college my head is spinning. What day is it? Which students are going to be there? And what is it that I teach?' The students, of course, have no idea of the other roles their lecturer has played in the course of the day. They simply see her as their teacher.

Lorene Noble, from Northern Queensland in Australia, writes: 'I have maintained my own work as a teacher wherever we have been, and have now taught every year level from kindergarten to final-year high school and also postgraduate university and in a wide range of subject areas. Had I not had to "reinvent" my own career through nineteen house moves I am certain it would not have been as diverse and enriching as it has been.' That is a typically positive spin on what could have been a hard situation. Lorene's gifts would almost certainly have taken her to the top of her profession had she been able to commit to staying in one place for long enough. But that is not mentioned. Instead, the rewards of variety are what she chooses to highlight.

Other spouses, too, have had varied working lives, finding opportunities wherever their nomadic lives lead them. Margaret Forsyth from Sydney, Australia, has managed to keep her piano teaching going through most of their moves, but has also worked 'as the manager of Arundel House, a hall of residence for female university students, close to the Sydney University campus. I now assist the CEO of a Baptist aged-care facility which administers a 76-bed nursing home and a 60-bed hostel.'

Diane Stanton, from Texas in the USA, works full-time as Executive Director of Uganda Christian University Partners, in an office based in her home. She, like all the others who wrote for me, also does a great variety of other things as well. Perhaps stamina and a love of variety are two of the key characteristics for a happy bishop's spouse!

Many bishops' spouses choose to work part-time, to make room for family and for supporting the bishop's ministry. Linda Baines, from Croydon in England, for example, works three days a week as a health visitor in a busy, multi-ethnic community. She has also, somehow, managed to complete an art degree, adding another string to her bow of ways of getting to know people.

Jo Cundy, from Peterborough in England, has 'worked in several solicitors' firms, mostly in a part-time capacity so as to have time for full involvement in home and church activities . . . Specializing in probate I enjoyed the opportunity I had in Sussex to develop a legacy campaign for the diocese.'

Jo is not alone in bringing the fruits of her professional qualifications to the work her husband does. Most spouses who work see what they do as valuable in its own right, but also as giving them insights into the community in which they live, which might not be immediately apparent from within the churchgoing world. Their work can help the bishop to understand his diocese better.

So many spouses would say that they work both to keep a sense of themselves and their own professional qualifications, and to bring a new dimension to their relationship with the diocese. But many also work out of sheer financial necessity. All clergy families know what it is like when people look at the houses we live in and assume we have the income to go with it. And I speak as someone who lives in two palaces! In fact, of course, bishops are not fabulously well paid, even in America and Britain, while in some other parts of the Anglican world their resources can be expected to stretch a very long way indeed.

Many bishops' spouses work in order to provide extra income for the family and for the diocese. Educating children is one of the biggest calls on the spouses' income, but several also use their resources to supplement training and welfare projects for other clergy families in the diocese.

For some bishops' spouses, this means that they have to work abroad. Comfort Fearon, from Nigeria, and Maria Akrofi, from Ghana, both hold down demanding jobs in Britain while playing a very full role in their husbands' ministries. Comfort writes: 'I live in two worlds and therefore live two lives.' The people who share each life know and understand little of the other part, which can make for a certain loneliness and dislocation.

Julia Flack, whose husband runs the work of the Anglican Church in Rome, writes, 'I never want to see Stansted airport ever again.' And other wives who face long-haul commutes also talk about the unreality of spending so much time in airports and planes, in a kind of no man's land. And when they arrive, they never quite belong in whichever half of their life they are in.

Although there are plenty of couples who work long distances apart, they are still unusual enough in church circles to provoke unkind gossip about the state of the marriage. Even when couples are fundamentally happy with the decisions they have made about their working lives, it is never easy to be apart for long periods of time, and ignorant and prurient gossip certainly doesn't help.

The working bishop's wife is becoming more and more of the norm, but the majority still feel they can only work part-time, because the Church does still seem to expect a lot from bishops' wives. (I am deliberately talking about 'wives' here – the situation is probably very different for bishops' husbands, as we shall see!) Although most bishops' wives say that their husbands are happy to help with shopping, cooking and child care, welcome and hospitality are very much at the heart of Christian ministry, and most wives want to be involved in that, too.

The sheer logistics of coping with two diaries and making themselves and their homes available to others does require great commitment. Many working bishops' wives do occasionally ask themselves if they are mad to be trying to do it all. But, on the whole, the ones who do go on working feel that to give up would drive them equally mad, and put other kinds of pressure on the household, either because of financial hardship or because of their own frustration.

That is certainly my own experience. Much as I love the people my husband is called to serve – or most of them! – it is his calling, not mine. My own calling is as a teacher and writer of theology, trying to make God more accessible to non-specialists. If I could not do this, I would feel that I was avoiding what God has asked me to do. I comfort myself with the reflection that Jesus called women to follow him, too. He never seems to have said that women could be disciples just by being good wives. Women have to make their own commitment to Christ. Of course, the same is true of men. Men are not fulfilling all God's requirements just by being good husbands. They, too, have to be disciples, and acknowledge God's calling as the primary thing in their lives. But most bishops' wives already know this, and arrange their lives around that fact.

In this need to accommodate the professional lives of two people, bishops' families are not very different from any others. The sheer normality of juggling two careers and a home and family may be an important part of the experience that a bishop and his wife share with the people they minister to.

And there are, of course, bishops who are not married and who yet manage to be as hospitable and welcoming as their married counterparts. And perhaps that should suggest that bishops' wives should let themselves off the hook a little and not feel so guilty about not fulfilling the role in exactly the way that previous generations of bishops' wives would have done.

Rebecca Cottrell
Reading (Oxford Diocese, England), married to Rt Revd Stephen Cottrell

Yesterday I attended my first ever meeting of bishops' wives up in London at Lambeth Palace. The meeting was mainly about the Lambeth Conference that would take place in the summer of 2008. In preparation for this we were all asked to write about what it is like being married to a bishop.

As I walked away from the meeting I thought to myself that I didn't have much to say on the subject. My life is so busy with everyday things. I am a full-time mother of three very active and fast-growing boys, who all have very hectic sport and social lives to which I am taxi driver par excellence, as we live in the middle of nowhere, with no public transport. I also have a part-time job as a session tutor, teaching pottery in a local college of further education. Consequently I do very little with my 'Bishop's Wife' hat on. (Yes, I do own a couple even though I didn't wear one at Stephen's consecration: this piece of information even reached the local press. Shock horror!) But as I travelled home I mulled all this through and decided that my story is just as valid. So here it is – a fairly typical day.

Wednesday 29 November 2006

I was woken by my alarm at 6 a.m., but didn't come to until 7. A bit too late, so I spent the next ten minutes waking and re-awaking my three boys. Stephen was making us a cup of tea before going into his study to say his morning prayers. The next half hour is pandemonium. Fighting, jostling and rolling down the stairs like lion cubs is how the youngest two greet the morning, while the eldest leaves it to the last minute to rise and shower. We make it to the kitchen to have breakfast together.

By 8 a.m. the boys have left the house to catch the school bus from the bottom of the road. I survey the mess and start to tidy up and vacuum the house. At 8.25 I get a frantic phone call. Sam my youngest is ringing from school to say he has food tech. this morning and has forgotten his ingredients, could I *please* take them in. I put the vacuum cleaner down, pick up my keys and grab the bag.

I decide that while I am down at the school I might as well do the shopping for tonight's dinner, so stop and get my purse. At this point Stephen reminds me that he has someone coming for lunch, and as I am going to the shops, could I buy some nice bread and cheese to go with the soup I am making.

I am back shortly after 9 a.m. As someone is coming for lunch I make a bigger effort of tidying the kitchen as it is there they will be eating. Even though I don't mind eating in a bit of a mess I didn't want a complete stranger doing the same. By just before 10 I have thoroughly spring-cleaned the kitchen and downstairs toilet. (Having three boys it is sometimes a half-hour mop out in there.) I jump into the car and go to Mass at our local church. This is the one bit of church in the week I do for myself. When I get back, the dog is sitting by the front door looking as though she hasn't had a walk for weeks, and how could I walk past and not take her out. I give in. We got the dog so that we would all enjoy the countryside where we live and to help Stephen get more exercise. I am not sure whether the rest of the family know where we keep her lead. Or that we live in the countryside!

Shopping done, house cleaned, dog walked, now time for me to get some of my work done. Lesson plans and assessments to write up. End-of-course reports to finish for this term and planning for next term. As I get into this the door bell rings and my brother-in-law arrives to deliver our new dining and coffee tables. He imports furniture, old and new, from India. I stop to admire them and thank him for the deal he has given us. (If anyone would like his contact number just email me!) Then back to work for a couple of hours.

I eat my lunch in the dining-room-cum-study while Stephen has his working lunch in the kitchen. Could do with a cup of tea but the kettle is in the kitchen and I am not sure how confidential their conversation is.

Three o'clock arrives and the boys are due home in fifteen minutes – just time to get off the computer so they can get their homework done. I teach an evening class on Wednesday evenings so Stephen tries to keep it free. But tonight he has something in his diary that he has to attend. This is a bit of a nightmare. On Wednesday evenings Sam has a piano lesson at 5.30 p.m. and then football practice at 6. I leave the football ground at 6.30 to get to work on time! From 5.30 to 10 I am out. Picking up, dropping off, getting to my class, teaching, then getting back home. Luckily it is only every other week that Joe, my eldest, has music theory from 4 to 4.30, otherwise I would be doing that as well today.

By the time I get to college my head is spinning. What day is it? Which students are going to be there? And what is it that I teach? The class goes really well, and by 10 p.m., when I get home (and find out the house hasn't burned down while I was out and Joe was babysitting), I make myself a cup of tea and collapse in a chair and unwind. Stephen and I chat a bit about the day. He has been meeting with local church leaders, trying to help a priest whose ministry has hit a difficult patch, planning mission strategy for the diocese (in the kitchen!) and taking a school assembly. A fairly typical day for him as well. As we talk he flicks aimlessly from one channel to the next trying to find something worth watching. We give in and go to bed.

There are a few extra roles that I do with my Bishop's Wife hat on. There is quite a lot of entertaining at home, and going to functions to support Stephen (babysitters permitting). But then there are also the perks. Being invited to openings of exhibitions; we went to one recently at the local museum, of the artist Stanley Spencer. Then there is of course being invited to watch Reading football team play at home!

I am sure that people in many different walks of life will read this and it will be very familiar. Being married to a bishop for me hasn't changed my life that much. Being married to Stephen has. It has always meant a life of fullness. A life packed to the brim and beyond; a life of excitement, changes and adventures. Throughout our life we have travelled many different roads together and this is just one more.

Comfort Fearon
Kaduna (Nigeria), married to the Most Revd Josiah Idowu-Fearon

How I became a Christian

I was born into a Christian family. Sunday was the day for going to church and we never missed no matter how tired. Saying prayers together as a family very early in the morning was what we got used to. As children, we never had a choice of whether we joined in the prayers or not. In 1972, I went to the nursing school far away from home and as someone who had always been in church, I joined the Christian Fellowship as well as the choir. It was during one of the services that I heard going to church didn't make one a Christian – I needed to take the step of accepting Jesus as my personal Saviour. This baffled me, but as I attended Bible study and read the Bible more, in June 1972, after further explanations, I accepted Jesus as my Lord and Saviour.

The effect my husband's election has had on my life

Being a clergy wife has a profound effect on one's life regardless of the position of the husband (i.e. vicar, archdeacon or bishop). I come from Nigeria where being a clergy wife means that some expectations are placed on you. You are meant to fit into this role and it is not a matter of choice. One is seen as the mother of all. You have to organize all women's programmes and take the leadership position. In this case, nobody prepares one for this position and nobody takes into account your level of education.

My husband's election as Bishop was meant to be a very joyous day, which it indeed was, and a day of promotion, but moving from a fairly affluent diocese to a newly created diocese with just the Bishop and three priests in a predominantly Muslim environment felt more like a demotion. As the Bishop's wife, I was now the 'mother' of the diocese since the Bishop was in charge of one. As we travelled around the diocese, the feeling inside me was that of intense mission work; the scenes I saw were so surprising. I could not believe this was the same Nigeria. Christians were in the minority and they were persecuted. Most of the Christians there were from the south of Nigeria and did not feel they were part of Sokoto State. Their allegiance was primarily where they originally came from. They had come all the way as government workers or traders.

My world had changed: three children who needed looking after, working full-time as a nurse, and the need to be involved fully in the Church, meant a struggle. Seeing the state of health care in the villages and around the diocese, I felt called to use my skills to start a rural health programme as well as work full-time in the hospital. The Bishop's time was taken up primarily with trying to raise funds, and searching for and training priests to fill the vacancies, which meant I did not see much of him.

Some of the local congregations had not seen a member of the clergy for a year, neither had they received communion. As Bishop in a predominantly Muslim community, there was need to foster good relationships with Muslims and this is still being promoted.

I also have to remember that my husband is not just the Bishop but is also the Archbishop of the province, which means being responsible for seven other dioceses. I have the job of looking after not just my diocese but the province. I look after all the bishops' wives and whatever difficulties they are having, as well as organize provincial activities. All of these have made an impact on my life.

How I spend my time and how it affects my faith

Sharing how I spend my time and how this affects my faith is a bit difficult. This is because I live in two worlds and therefore live two lives. Part of me lives in Nigeria where I spend a lot of time leading and teaching women and being involved in a lot of diocesan activities. Here, I spend my time sharing my faith all the time and helping others to take the step of committing their lives to Christ; helping those caught up in various day-to-day issues women face and seeing life-changing experiences helps to cement my faith. As the 'mother' of the diocese, people find it easy to confide in me and I find myself counselling all the time. This is a very humbling experience but can be quite demanding. I also feel privileged to be involved in the lives of people.

In my other life in the UK, I spend the greater part of my time working in order to educate the children. In the UK, things are very different and sharing one's faith is not as easy as it is at home. The liberal attitude to faith means that colleagues at work don't understand what you are trying to say, and you are often branded as 'religious'. Sharing faith with patients is frowned upon unless they volunteer, which is quite rare.

Lorene Noble
North Queensland (Australia), married to
Rt Revd John Noble

I was baptized as an infant in a then Church of England (now Anglican) church, in Brisbane, Queensland, in Australia, but attended a Presbyterian church with a friend as we could walk there. Consequently, from these earliest years I have known the value of 'being and having a friend'. However, once our family had a car, we connected with the local Church of England again and, as a young teenager, I joined a Sunday group called Companionship. It had a series of study units preparing one for Christian living, but what I see now was that it was not the content that mattered so much but the wisdom and witness of the layperson who mentored us. This, I believe, has been the foundation for my Christian formation and growth – there seem always to have been people with whom I have connected who have guided me, sometimes in very small and seemingly insignificant ways to them, I am sure, but with what turned out to be life-changing experiences for me.

In 1969 I married John and our time together has brought such varied experiences. He was ordained when we married but I continued to work as a high school teacher so he could train to become a teacher, too. He practised as a teacher, then as a school chaplain, a parish priest, a theological college lecturer, and then as a bishop, first as a regional bishop, then as one responsible for diocesan Christian education, then as a diocesan bishop. He is about to return to parish ministry because his health cannot sustain the travel demands of this diocese. Our current diocese is 2000 km by 1000 km in size, with many scattered centres and diverse needs and with widespread indigenous ministry as well as three large coastal cities, 800 km apart to the north and south of Townsville where we live, and, 1000 km west, a large mining centre.

The involvements in a variety of activities that these varying placements have brought for me have certainly been a challenge, demanding a need to grow myself in many capacities. At times, they have also brought sheer physical fatigue, as I have driven thousands of kilometres and sometimes lived in homes that were totally unsuitable for the ministry we were in and where little support was available. However, they have also brought contact with a wide variety of people and many shared experiences that I believe are unique to the work my husband is involved in. The need to encourage people in their Christian walk is ever present and especially needed where people are isolated or experiencing demanding working and living conditions.

I have maintained my own work as a teacher wherever we have been, and have now taught every year level from kindergarten to final-year high school and also postgraduate university and in a wide range of subject areas. Had I not had to 'reinvent' my own career through nineteen house moves I am certain it would not have been as diverse and enriching as it has been, and I also believe our children have benefited from learning to adapt to new situations as they now pursue their adult lives, which have seen them moving around the globe. My faith has been stretched often, but the need to rely on the Lord solely when we faced situations where we knew no one initially has only strengthened my personal relationship with and reliance on my Lord and the consciousness of the daily infilling of the Holy Spirit. As I was mentored wisely along the way, I trust I have been available in this capacity for others, too, as we bring the good news of our Lord in whatever situation we find ourselves.

5

Minority report

————◆◆◆————

In most of the Anglican Communion, bishops and their spouses have a certain status. Many are slightly uncomfortable about that, both because they are not sure how Christian it is, and because they suspect that it is often based on misconceptions about what their lives are really like. I am sure that I am not alone in suffering occasionally from a quite interesting dissonance between what I realize my life must look like from the outside and what it actually feels like from the inside. I have the enormous privilege of dressing up occasionally to go to Buckingham Palace, of teaching about God's option for the poor, and of trying to stretch the budget to all that a family of four living in central London needs. Neither my husband nor I were born to this, or even aspired to it, so it is odd to be treated with such curiosity. Ours is just a rather exaggerated form of something that many bishops' families would recognize. Ask any bishop's child, and they will tell you that school friends automatically assume they are 'posh'.

There are all kinds of historical reasons why bishops and their families are thought to be a certain 'class'. Most of them probably were until comparatively recently. When most Anglican bishops came, at least originally, from the Church of England, and most Church of England bishops were educated at Oxford and Cambridge, and most Oxford- and Cambridge-educated people came from the moneyed classes, it is easy to see how episcopacy and class seemed to fit together. Thankfully, each of those stages on the way to the end result has changed, so that bishops in the Anglican Church worldwide are generally neither English nor Oxbridge-educated nor moneyed.

But the idea of the bishop's status still seems to survive. It is also possible that some of this assumed 'status' is nothing to do with class structures and everything to do with respect for a Christian leader. Let's hope so. And that kind of respect is still given to bishops and church leaders in parts of the world where there is no historical association between class and episcopacy.

It is particularly moving to see that respect offered to bishops in parts of the world where to be a Christian at all is automatically to be of low status, and to diminish your chances of getting a good education or a good job or any of the other things by which society measures worth. Christians under those circumstances can genuinely honour each other for their witness and their role in the Christian community.

But if it is hard enough to be a Christian at all in certain societies, it can be even harder to be a bishop, both because recognized leaders may be targeted when the Christian community is under attack, and because the paternal and protective role of the bishop becomes even more important and demanding under such circumstances.

I met the wife of the previous Anglican bishop in Iran some years ago. She spoke little about their lives, but it was clear that they lived in great tension. Her husband was the only remaining bishop in Iran, so his workload was immense. Yet his freedom of movement was severely restricted and his security far from guaranteed. For a number of years after he retired, there was no Anglican bishop in Iran. When at last a bishop from Pakistan was given permission to take Iran under his wing, he was moved at the welcome he received from faithful Christians. People received communion with tears of joy streaming down their faces, and he performed marathon confirmation services for all those who had been unable to make their adult commitment to the Church in the absence of a bishop.

His wife is proud of the joy and service that her husband is able to bring to Iran, but the family dynamic is not easy. Her husband has to be away a lot, and, even though the bishop has permission to be in Iran, he is not necessarily the most welcome of visitors, as far as the authorities are concerned. Inevitably, such a ministry requires wife and family to set aside some of their natural fears to set the bishop free to accept his calling.

Elizabeth San San Htay, from Toungoo in Myanmar, also knows what it is to worry about the safety of her husband. Toungoo has many internally displaced persons in the diocese, people who have had to leave their own homes because of armed conflict or unrest, and who are very dependent upon their fellow Christians for care and support. She writes of these people: 'They have been hiding, moving, displacing, longing and crying for peace and prosperity for years and years. It is not very safe for John [her husband] to travel and visit villages.'

But he does it, whether it is safe or not, because a bishop must care for the flock. Under these circumstances, Elizabeth has discovered her own calling to prayer. 'Prayer is the most important thing in my life as a bishop's spouse.' Clearly, for Elizabeth and her fellow Christians, prayer is not a passive thing, for they have also managed, despite the restrictions placed on Christian activity and building projects, to set up provision for 'health care for villagers, sanitation and water supplies for villages, education for children from remote areas and communities, vocational training and programmes for young people and communities of other faiths'. All of which sounds positively miraculous, considering the circumstances.

In Pakistan, too, the Christian Church is called to be with the poorest of the poor. Many of the Christians in Pakistan are from the lowest echelons of society, and even those who have intelligence and education find it hard to get jobs in civil society. Christians are very much on the margins of the way Pakistan understands itself and its citizens. It is a Muslim country, and even those Christians who were born and brought up in Pakistan, and whose families go back several generations, are aware that they are not really thought of as properly Pakistani.

Benita Rumalshah, the wife of the Bishop of Peshawar, is herself Indian by birth, and found it hard to adjust to the much more restricted position of women in Pakistan. Women are generally quite segregated, and expected to be well covered when they do go out. 'The realization that to be a woman among these people was to live behind closed doors disturbed me to my very core,' Benita writes.

Most of the bishops' wives from Pakistan whom I spoke to said that the way women and girls are treated is one of their major concerns, because of the practical consequences for their own congregations. Because so many Christian families are poor, a lot of the girls become maids or servants in wealthy non-Christian households, where they are not infrequently subjected to physical and sexual abuse. Both because of their poverty and lack of influence, and because of their 'outsider' status in society, there is very little hope of legal redress for these girls. Those who have been raped are routinely disbelieved by police authorities, even supposing they are brave enough to make a complaint in the first place. They also become 'spoiled goods' as far as their marriage prospects are concerned.

Most of the bishops' wives I spoke to in Pakistan were routinely involved in rape counselling, in social projects for the care and rehabilitation of the poor, in work with prostitutes, in literacy projects and in a whole range of other things for which they had no training except experience and prayer. Few of them would have offered themselves for such work but they shoulder it bravely and uncomplainingly as part of their sharing in their husbands' ministries.

Relations between Muslims and Christians are by no means universally bad in Pakistan, and there are salutary lessons to be learned by those of us who live in countries where Christianity is taken to be the norm and Muslims and those of other faiths are made to feel like 'outsiders'. One of the key questions for us as bishops' spouses at the Lambeth Conference will be how to hear each other's experience of living and working with people of other faiths in ways that will be constructive rather than angry.

Inevitably, that will look very different for those who have 'converted' from other religions, or who know the dynamic of interfaith tension within their own families. Lily Lai, from Taiwan, remembers being beaten as a child when she started to be interested in Christianity. Like most people in Taiwan, her family practised a mixture of folk religion, Taoism and Buddhism, and it took courage and luck for Lily to be able to become a Christian. 'It is only by the grace of God that I can write these words now, as I look back on my journey to faith and its most unlikely and seemingly impossible start.' Lily's life makes her particularly suited to the work which Taiwan is uniquely equipped to do, which is providing a bridge between America and Asia. Taiwan is officially a diocese in the Episcopal Church of America, but has very close links with Asia, too. Lily knows all about bridges from one people and one mindset to another.

Relations with people of other faiths and other practices are never easy, but the situation Christianity is in now is by no means new. After all, the Christian faith started out as a minority religion, so there should be nothing alien to us in this situation. It started out as a religion that appealed particularly to the marginalized – one early Roman commentator on Christianity called it, sneeringly, a 'religion of slaves and women'. It is not, in its heart, well designed for the ruling classes, with its subversive critique of power and its preaching of the God incarnate and crucified. Jesus shows us God's heart and God's image of power, as he washes the feet of his disciples and as he submits to the pain and humiliation of the cross. Those of us who are able to live comfortable Christian lives have a lot to learn from our sisters in Pakistan, Taiwan and Myanmar.

Benita Rumalshah
Peshawar (Pakistan), married to Rt Revd Mano Rumalshah

My heritage is from a Christian family of West Bengal in India. My great-grandparents crossed the threshold of faith to Christianity which, according to my grandfather, offered him a whole new vision of godhead. I was nurtured in the richness of that Hinduized culture and within its experience with the distinctiveness of the Christian faith. My journey of faith in those formative years helped me to see the place of faith in every breath of my life and the realization that our life on earth is simply a pilgrimage with our destiny in the omega point.

My encounter with the wider world began when in my late twenties I was offered a teaching post in Australia under the Commonwealth Teachers' Programme, which eventually landed me in England. It is here only that I got married to a priest of Pakistani origin (loving your enemy). We got settled into the groove of living in a vicarage in our adopted Church and country of England. There was not much thought about returning to our roots, partly because we became quite cosy and comfortable and as we were from India and Pakistan we knew that it would be extremely difficult for us to find a home in either of these countries.

However, a day of reckoning dawned upon us and the moment of truth had arrived to challenge us. We were invited to serve in the North-West Frontier Province of Pakistan, bordering a lawless zone with Afghanistan. We knew that the area includes the famous Khyber Pass and that it is the setting for *The Far Pavilions* and some romantic Hollywood movies.

We accepted the challenge and landed in this region almost twenty years ago. At the time of our leaving I was a college lecturer in Chelsea, London. Having been brought up in India, I felt as a woman that I was being thrown into an abyss. To add spice to the situation, even my husband was equally foreign to the area; he was totally ignorant of the culture and language of these tribal Pakhtoons.

It is in such a world that my husband was called to become the third Bishop of Peshawar in 1994. This was a momentous step in our lives because it was obvious that now there would be no 'going back home'. The jurisdiction of the diocese spans the whole of the province, with a population of about sixteen million and with a sprinkling of about ten thousand Christians spread in the far reaches of the area. Church in such a hostile and fundamentalist place became very demanding as our people not only were marginalized but also extremely poor and the majority were simply menial workers.

My own identity and perception changed alarmingly as I found myself to be the 'First Lady' without any deep knowledge of the culture and especially the language. The realization that to be a woman among these people was to live behind closed doors disturbed me to my very core. I had to rediscover my inner strength and create a place for myself with a new sense of responsibility and purpose.

This kind of situation inevitably leads you into a new realm of discovery and service. This led me to offer myself to the ministry of hospitality and encouragement. I suffer from the same syndrome as most other 'episcopal widows'. My husband travels excessively both within the diocese and outside it. Like any housewife and mother in a similar situation I keep the episcopal household going and also offer all the support that I can to those who come to us 'looking for the Bishop'. Such a kind of ministry has its own ups and downs but it always engages you with people. It is because of this particular situation that my contribution may seem to be not only to the women but to all people.

In this part of the world, faith plays a crucial role in our day-to-day living. Being the minority we cannot emphasize enough the importance of having regular worship together to share, to meet to revive our belief. As families we encounter each other, we share our joys and sorrows; we know that we are together in our struggle. Love of our Lord infuses us with warmth and power. We share with others in God's wondrous work to serve people who are Christian, as well as people of other faiths, through education, health-care centres, and through outreach such as community development programmes. Our everyday witness to people of God is through *diakonia*, work for others. Recently, we have been trying to educate our families about problems that are new. Our effort is to make them aware of these and not to pretend that they don't exist but to be equipped to tackle them wisely and patiently.

We thank God for our experiences abroad which enriched our contacts in the western world. Our unique experience and opportunity can help us to build bridges for people of both East and West. We wanted to be counted here and now. Our foreign contacts were bold enough to venture out in this land of ours which is fraught with many dangers. This is a place where life and death go hand in hand. One is thankful to be alive and doing God's will here because the next moment one might be attacked or taken hostage or may even be shot at. As we are here, our friends across the world take interest and come out here to meet us. Thereby we portray the catholicity of our faith. It is so heartening to feel that we are *one body* in Christ.

May God accept us, unworthy as we are, yet make us that channel through which he might flow to rejuvenate and recreate us all.

As my bishop uncle (who was the first indigenous diocesan Bishop of North India during the British Raj) wrote: 'We believe that like an incense stick we are burning for Him. The fragrance scatters itself all around us and to all God's people. At the end the ashes will gather at the feet of our blessed Lord!'

My humble prayer is: may we always be that 'incense stick' that burns for him in this broken and despised world.

Elizabeth San San Htay
Toungoo (Myanmar), married to Rt Revd John Wilme

I was born and brought up in a Barmer Christian family. I loved to go to church with my parents when I was a child, and to Sunday school with my sisters and brother. I served as a Sunday school teacher for more than five years when I was a young person in my own parish, called St Michael's Church.

I had completed four years of theological studies at Holy Cross Theological College, Yangon, and then served as lecturer there for eight years and as Director of the Christian Education Department of Yangon Diocese, until we moved to Toungoo when John was elected to be Diocesan Bishop of Toungoo in 1994.

It was very hard for me to leave my job and move to a different place with my husband. It took years for me to stop crying after the election. Finally I learned and discovered that we are called to serve the Living God who loves us so much in this particular region, Toungoo Diocese.

Toungoo Diocese is the largest diocese in the province in terms of membership. Many of them are internally displaced persons because of the conflict between armed groups. They have been hiding, moving, displacing, longing and crying for peace and prosperity for years and years. It is not very safe for John to travel and visit villages. Therefore, prayer is the most important thing in my life as a bishop's spouse. Thank God that, despite various difficulties and restrictions, we provided and are providing health care for villagers, sanitation and water supplies for villages, education for children from remote areas and communities, vocational training and programmes for young people and communities of other faiths.

Being a spouse I am very happy to serve and offer my gifts as president of the Mothers' Union and the YWCA of Toungoo, teaching at St Peter's Bible School, supervising diocesan pre-schools and Dorcas' sewing and craft centre, as an advisor to the Men's Association, Anglican Young People's Association and Christian Education Committee.

All these experiences help me to pray and study the living words of God more in my daily life. They help me to understand more about my calling. I have learned that God's purpose is always beyond our very limited knowledge and he has always a special plan for me to promote his Kingdom, especially in this diocese filled with hardships and difficulties. Being a spouse is not an easy life but it is really a joy to serve the Lord through sharing my gifts with John, who has been Diocesan Bishop for thirteen years in Toungoo, which covers more than a hundred villages with about twenty thousand baptized members who are struggling with daily survival, together with thirty-five clergy and ninety-six catechists.

Joy (1 Peter 4.12–19) was the theme of 2007 for all of us in Toungoo Diocese.

Ma Myint Myint Yee
Hpa-an (Myanmar), married to
Rt Revd Stephen Than Myint Oo

I am a third-generation Christian and was baptized when I was a month old. That is to say I became a Christian when I was a month old. Yet my Christian faith was nurtured by the Anglican Church in Myanmar and I had my confirmation when I was about 16 years old. To be able to live as Christians among non-Christians, who are the majority in our place, our Christian faith must be strong.

I grew up as a village girl working in the paddy fields and farms. But God called me to serve him by sending me to an Anglican Bible school, called Emmanuel Divinity School, which is located in Upper Myanmar, when I was 20 in 1979. After finishing my theological studies, I served as the head of the Religious Education Department in Mandalay Diocese, which is located in Middle Myanmar.

I married Mr Stephen Than Myint Oo in 1986. My husband served in the provincial office of the Church of the Province of Myanmar in Lower Myanmar. We therefore had to be separated from each other for two years. Then I quit my job and came to my husband so that we could live together. We had to separate from each other again – for the next four years – when my husband enrolled as a student at Holy Cross Theological College so that he could serve as a priest in our province. This frequent separation gave me a great pain in my heart. I had to look after my three sons – Sa Sai Naw Aye, Sa Shine Luka and Michael Wine Mya San – without my husband for about four years.

My husband became a priest in 1994 and we had the chance to live together again. He was both a lecturer at Holy Cross Theological College and a priest in charge of a church. He was, therefore, a very busy person and he could not spend much time with his own family. Hence I had to struggle hard for my family. It was the practice in our culture that religious persons – clergy or lay – should not pay much attention to their families. Insufficient salary and income made our struggle harder. However, I was very happy to be a priest's wife because it is the calling of God to serve God as a priest's wife and I value it very much.

My husband seemed not to tire in serving the Lord and he always encouraged me. He often told me not to be discouraged and told me that we had to keep our hearts pure in every circumstance. He also reminded me to be ready to face everything for Christ.

Our house was always filled with visitors from the villages who came to town for various purposes, church members and students. So I had to serve them. On the other hand, I had to look after my three sons because we did not have any servant or housekeeper. All this made me very tired. But in my tiredness I saw many wonderful things that God had done for us.

Unexpectedly, my husband was elected as the Bishop of the Diocese of Hpa-an in 2005. I was shocked and I had a dual feeling – happy and worried. I was happy because my husband had become a bishop and it was a mark of God's acknowledgement for his sacrificial ministry. I was worried because I knew that the demands and responsibilities of the role of a bishop are much greater than those of a priest.

My feelings came true when we moved to the diocese in which my husband was to serve. Within a year I realized that my husband's hair had become white. Sometimes he looked very tense. So I decided to spend more time with my husband – to accompany him wherever he went, sometimes just sitting quietly beside him when he sank into his deep thought and so on. I thank God for enabling me to act on my decision because my three sons are growing up now – the eldest one is 18, the middle one 15, the youngest one 13.

I therefore have more time to serve as the president of the Mothers' Union of our diocese – especially with the sewing project, looking after the poor, visiting the sick, prayer services and so on – while assisting my husband. The more I have time to serve in MU work and to assist my husband, the more I feel that my energy to serve the Lord increases. It is indeed the blessing of God being a bishop's wife for I have found the goodness, faithfulness and greatness of God in the demanding work and challenging task of a bishop and his family.

To God be the glory.

6

Reader, I married her

In 1989 Barbara Harris was consecrated as Assisting (Suffragan) Bishop of Massachusetts, America. She was the first woman bishop in the Anglican Church. Since then, two other provinces of the Anglican Church, New Zealand and Canada, have consecrated women to the episcopate, though a number of others have passed the necessary legislation to enable that to happen. Women bishops are not yet commonplace, but their presence is increasingly taken for granted, and seems to be becoming less controversial. Inevitably, there remain some Anglicans who are theologically opposed to women's ordination at all, let alone their consecration as bishops, but it is perhaps instructive to note that when, in 2006, Katharine Jefferts Schori was elected as Presiding Bishop of the Episcopal Church in America, those who opposed her election mostly did so on the grounds of her views on sexuality, rather than because of her gender.

Eleven women bishops were present at the last Lambeth Conference, in 1998, and some of them brought husbands with them, necessitating a 'spouses' conference' rather than a 'wives' conference'.

But while there has been much written and said about the experience of women bishops, there has been less about their husbands' perceptions of life. Women bishops join an overwhelmingly male environment, where most of their role models, past and present, are male. They are aware that some people want them to model something a bit different, while others are waiting to pounce on any perceived deviation from the norm. They face loneliness, sexism, marginalization and a great deal of projection, as well as warmth, welcome, hope and a simple expectation that they will just get on with the job.

Most of the time, their husbands will not have to be quite so conscious of joining the largely female company of episcopal spouses.

They will have their own work peers and their own lives. But bishops' husbands, although few and far between, were very noticeable at Lambeth 1998, and were welcomed with what must have been an uncomfortable mixture of joy, amusement, curiosity and shyness. No doubt Lambeth 2008 will be very similar.

The experience of being the husband of a bishop is very different from that of being the wife of a bishop. Of course, there are some things in common, like not being able to sit with one's spouse in church, or take holidays at Christmas and Easter. Or the more serious and painful experience of being married to someone whose job routinely involves being the butt of anger and childish tantrums. Bishops, whatever their sex, are automatically blamed for all perceived wrongs in the Church, and seldom praised for any of its virtues. When a deeply ingrained misogyny is added to the mix, it must make it even harder to bear, and harder to stand by and witness on behalf of one's spouse. Frederick Quinn, the husband of the Bishop of Utah, has had to learn that he can only make life more difficult for his wife if he attempts to defend her.

Frederick Quinn and his wife are both ordained. This is not unknown – there are several clerical couples where the husband is a bishop and the wife a priest. But the Quinns are, at the moment, very unusual. The kind of issues raised by women priests whose husbands are bishops tend to relate to deployment and boundaries between professional and private life. When is your husband your 'father in God' and when is he your husband? When you need a 'father in God' who is not also your husband, where do you go? Presumably the issues are the same when the bishop is the wife. The innate conservatism of some Christian communities allied with a theology of male headship may complicate the situation for a woman bishop with a priest husband, but this is an area where role models outside the Church may help. We are increasingly used to seeing women in positions of authority and most clergy and lay people are now used to working with senior women colleagues both in the Church and in the rest of their working lives.

Husbands of bishops, like wives, have to face moving house and leaving friends when God calls. But it is probably easier for the husband of a bishop to be lonely. Bishops' wives can easily be members of a clergy spouses' association which will be largely female, as well as other women's organizations, widely found in Anglican churches around the world. Men tend to be less well provided for, and with far fewer people of similar experience close by.

There must be all kinds of advantages to the fact that husbands of bishops face fewer expectations of what they will do in support of their spouses than wives do. Presumably, husbands are not expected to cater for large gatherings, do the flowers, convene the Mothers' Union and generally be a mother to the diocese as a whole. Many bishops' wives are very uncomfortable with this kind of expectation, which they feel does not necessarily fit their own gifts. But such expectations can at least bring some shape and some ready-made community to a bishop's wife, which may well be lacking for a husband.

If more of the eleven provinces who have given theoretical consent to women as bishops start to put that into practice, the phenomenon of the bishop's husband should become more commonplace in ways that might make it easier. It is also possible that more bishops' husbands will make life easier for bishops' wives, too, as the mismatch of expectations when the bishop has a husband and when the bishop has a wife becomes more obvious.

Who knows what the scene will look like by Lambeth 2018?

Frederick Quinn
Utah (USA), married to Rt Revd Carolyn Tanner Irish

In a hurried baptismal service near the front door of a church following the main Sunday service decades ago, unbeknownst to me, I became a Christian. I have been trying to live into the meaning of baptism ever since. A lodestar has been the Baptismal Covenant of the American Book of Common Prayer (1982), with its provision to 'strive for justice and peace among all people, and respect the dignity of every human being'.

Becoming a Christian was an unfolding process. Raised in an Irish Roman Catholic working-class setting in rural Pennsylvania, I became a Unitarian in college, attracted by that tradition's respect for intellectual inquiry and racial and social justice issues. But Anglicanism was never absent from my horizon, represented by the cadenced language of the Book of Common Prayer and the thoughtful explanations of the local rector in the town where I attended college. I did not have a conversion experience, but one night in 1956 I returned home from the night shift at a newspaper in Meadville, Pennsylvania, and by chance played a recording of an Advent Lessons and Carols Service from King's College, Cambridge. A solitary treble sang, 'I looked from afar, and, lo, I saw the power of God coming . . .'. I said softly to myself, 'There is *really* something here worth exploring', and listened to the record over several days.

I was also fascinated by Søren Kierkegaard and had read an essay on the Danish writer by Howard A. Johnson, canon theologian at the Cathedral of St John the Divine in New York City. I visited Johnson, who was immensely busy but who freely offered me a weekly tutorial in historic Anglican thought for the few months I lived in New York. It was also the beginning of Lent and from the cathedral services I experienced the changing musical and liturgical expressions of the church year. When the cathedral's great bronze doors opened on a misty Easter morning and the State Trumpet stop thundered out 'Jesus Christ is risen today' as a congregation of thousands sang, I knew in my heart the resurrection was true.

For three decades I worked as an American Foreign Service Officer in Africa, Asia, the Caribbean, and Central Europe, increasingly focusing on issues of constitutional reform and human rights. I was also ordained midway during a Foreign Service career in 1975 in Washington DC, and remained bivocationally active for many years as a priest in several parishes of the Diocese of Washington, and as Anglican chaplain in Prague (1975–78) and Warsaw (1993–95).

Since Carolyn was elected tenth Bishop of Utah in 1995 and we were not married until the summer of 2001, after the death of my first wife, her election had no immediate effect on me. However, being an active male priest married to a woman bishop presented unique challenges, including a move from Washington DC's National Cathedral, where I was active as a chaplain, leaving a close community of friends, and a culturally and intellectually stimulating setting, for Salt Lake City, Utah.

Loneliness is a challenge. I am rarely asked to preach, teach or celebrate the Eucharist in Utah and have minimal contact with diocesan clergy and laity. Fortunately, there are frequent invitations to write, speak and participate in professional consultations elsewhere.

Misogyny is another issue – difficult because as a male spouse I have no voice if the Bishop is being attacked by a male, or on occasion female, priest. Misogyny is widespread in the Church but rarely discussed, even as women increasingly move into positions of power and authority. Misogyny follows a distinct pattern: the attacker's intent is to make a woman cry in public or become angry and lose face. The unspoken assumption is the victim will remain silent and not call attention to the attack. Misogynists also make direct confrontation difficult through using carefully veiled language.

At one local church meeting, when the attacker's ugly words and aggressive body language had ended, he turned, winked at me and asked how I was enjoying life in a new town. I wanted to slam him against the wall, but didn't. In such a setting, both my first wife (in the Foreign Service) and second wife (in the Church) understandably said, 'I must solve the problem in my way; if you intervene, people would think I couldn't handle it.'

Note to the Primates: when you finish with sex, add misogyny to your short list of behavioural issues for communiqués and covenants.

Life is good and joyful. We have a loving relationship, travel through a spectacularly beautiful state, and the welcome of small churches is heartfelt in places like Vernal, Whiterocks, Ogden and Provo. Their potluck dinners are a foretaste of the celestial banquet, their generous sharing of resources an example of the Beatitudes in action. My Bible is filled with cherished notes received from such parish encounters here and elsewhere during a thirty-year ministry.

There are humorous moments as well. The Latter-Day Saints Church has over three thousand male bishops. When Carolyn was elected Bishop of Utah, Episcopalians distributed a bumper sticker, 'Honk if your bishop is a woman'. Never lacking in humour, a similar 'Honk if your woman is a bishop' bumper sticker was given to me by the congregation of St John's, Logan.

As for how I spend my own time, I like to write and sing. I take a weekly singing lesson, and present an annual Washington programme with a Jewish woman psychotherapist on religious themes in the works of various composers. Law, history or religion are the subjects of the books I have published so far, *The Image of Islam and Muslims in Western Thought* (Oxford University Press, 2007) being the most recent. Presently I am writing about the religious issues of globalization: the book's working title is *The House with Many Rooms*. This is an exciting time for Anglicans to look closely at issues of religious pluralism and the variety of daily interactions, beliefs and spiritual practices within various religious traditions. Theology is no longer the province of dead white men speaking German. Especially in Asia, a new generation of women writers on Christianity is producing heartfelt commentaries deeply illuminating about faith journeys. This is the subject matter I am seeking to make sense of as priest, historian and diplomat of thirty years.

Richard Schori
(USA), married to the Most Revd Katharine Jefferts Schori, Presiding Bishop of the US Episcopal Church

I am a cradle Episcopalian and have been active in church life for most of my life. The exception was when I was a graduate student in mathematics and became a passionate rock-climber, spending my weekends either in the crags or studying mathematics. My main interest in church life has to do with building community. I am not theologically trained but have a long history of knowing and befriending well-known priests and bishops even before meeting my wife.

I want to start the discussion about how Katharine's election as a bishop affected my life at the point when she became a priest. This had not been in my life plan since when I married Katharine she was a shy graduate student in oceanography and neither of us had any idea that she would go in this direction. We met at a stewardship dinner at the Episcopal church in Corvallis, Oregon, soon after I arrived there as chair of the department of mathematics at Oregon State University. We married a year later in 1979 and it was a good ten years later that she started seriously thinking of going to seminary. At the time, my first reaction was that I could not imagine myself going around with someone wearing a 'collar'. However, as an adaptable human being, I soon became comfortable with this, partly because we continued to live in our home town where I had my own job, activities and friends.

Some years later I found myself being stretched again when there was talk of her being a candidate for Bishop of Nevada. This wasn't in my life plan either, but guess what, she was elected. My life has seldom been boring but this put a whole new direction to it. First, an eye-opening idea was that I was able to retire, a definite advantage of being older than Katharine. I had experienced success as a research mathematician, sportsman and father, and did not mind retiring at all. However, moving to a large city from our comfortable community in Oregon was difficult. I'm quite extroverted and my friends and organizations in Oregon were hard to give up. Actually, I have gone back to Oregon quite a few times to maintain my contacts there.

After five years of community-building in Nevada, I began to feel at home and liked my lifestyle of tennis, travel, friends, teaching a web-based calculus course, and volunteer website work. Also, my years of growing up in a family consisting mostly of women was paying dividends as I felt comfortable with our active bishops' spouses organization, consisting mostly of women. My digital picture-taking and my placing of them on websites was gratifying and appreciated.

Now, don't you think this would be enough? I've always prided myself on being an adventurer, as most dramatically evidenced by my significant rock-climbing and high mountain adventures throughout the United States and ten foreign countries, and I wasn't looking for more. Now I was being pushed again when Katharine became a candidate for, and then elected as, Presiding Bishop and Primate of the Episcopal Church. This was epitomized when she called me immediately after being elected saying, 'I got elected, and I'm so glad you are an adventurer.'

I'm slowly figuring out the implications of being the PBS (Presiding Bishop Spouse), and it is looking like the biggest jump discontinuity (mathematical term) yet. I am an admitted extrovert, but I've always valued having the ability of going off anonymously by myself or with friends and this is becoming much more difficult. On the other hand, I'm travelling more now and meeting a wider and more influential circle of people. To do this takes serious study of schedules to see what activities make sense for me. This is not easy as I'm trying to maintain our home in Nevada, a 'long-term' cabin in Oregon, and a lovely apartment in New York. But, basically, I am awed by this huge, huge opportunity in life that very few people will have. It is something that I had no expectations of, nor aspirations for, but here I am feeling wondrously blessed and humbled. My prayer is that I can be a worthy servant to our Church, the Anglican Communion and our world.

Finally, I'd like to say something about my roots. My last name, Schori, is of Swiss-German origins but in fact I am 75 per cent English. Some of the names in my family are Haley, Webb, Chase, Wheeler, Robinson and Miles (my middle name). I lived for a summer in Kenilworth, Warwickshire, a village a few miles south of Coventry, England, when I was a visiting professor at the University of Warwick. I am very proud of my English ancestry and visited the grave site of my great-great-great-grandparents John and Sarah Robinson in Olney, Buckinghamshire.

7

To Lambeth

On 16 July 2008 bishops and their spouses from all over the world will converge on Canterbury. For nearly three weeks, we will worship and work together to try to hear God's calling to the Anglican Church.

At the heart of the Christian understanding of church is the belief that although God calls us as individuals, he calls us to be together. Just as God is Trinity, Father, Son and Holy Spirit, and cannot be known properly just as 'God', so Christians cannot be understood rightly if seen in isolation.

That is why it is not a luxury for Christian leaders to meet together. It is a simple necessity. Local churches and their leaders will inevitably only grasp a little of what God is saying to the whole Church. We need to meet to piece together the individual fragments that have been given to us to make a coherent whole.

Throughout the history of the Christian Church, there have been 'ecumenical councils'. Ecumenical means 'from all over the world'. These councils have never been calm occasions where all Christians speak with one voice. The earliest recorded council is described in Acts 15, where Christian leaders gathered to discuss the highly tendentious issue of whether all Christian converts had to follow certain Jewish practices. This crisis reverberates not only through the pages of the New Testament, but also through the writings of a number of the Christian leaders of the first few centuries of the Christian Church. The writer of Acts feels that things came to some kind of a resolution by the end of the Jerusalem council he describes, but that council clearly was not felt to be the end of the matter as far as all Christians were concerned from then on.

The Lambeth Conference of 2008 will also see differences of opinion on major matters of faith and practice. But that is exactly why it has to happen. If we cannot listen to each other, and hear why people respond to God's call in their own situation as they do, then we will not serve our world at all well.

The theme of the conference is to be 'God's people for God's mission'. Tempting as it is simply to dwell on our own internal problems, all Christian leaders are aware that there is no such thing as 'internal problems' for the Church. Everything we are and do affects how we present God to the rest of the world, and since that is all the Church exists for – to celebrate and preach God – we cannot afford the luxury of being inward-looking.

Although the main body of the conference will consist of bishops and their spouses, there will be representatives of all kinds of Christian organizations there, to inform, to share and to bear witness to the reality of the Anglican Church.

The spouses' conferences are a comparatively recent addition to the Lambeth Conference. No doubt wives came along to every conference, but their role was not acknowledged as needing examination or support until a few decades ago. Despite the financial climate and the tension within the Anglican Communion, there was no hesitation this time around about the need for a spouses' conference. I hope this book will have given pause to those of you who had doubts about the wisdom of that. The simple fact is that bishops' spouses do an incredible amount in the service of the bishops' ministries and they, too, need to meet together and seek God's truth in their combined experience and their combined listening to God.

We will spend some time on issues that particularly relate to us as spouses. For example, how we feel about perceptions of us; how we cope when the role doesn't seem to fit us; how we manage the public/private divide in our lives. We will also make time to meet in regional groups. In some parts of the Anglican Communion lack of money and difficulty of travel make it impossible for bishops' spouses to meet regularly, so the Lambeth Conference will make it possible for people in local regions to consult each other, sometimes for the first time.

Then we will think about what kind of support families need in our changing world. Not just bishops' families, but all families are under pressure, and where families don't work, neither does society. All bishops' spouses come with experience of supporting families in need, both clergy families and others.

There will be other issues that particularly affect women around the world, such as rape, domestic violence and HIV/AIDS. Many of these issues will be shared sessions between bishops and spouses, since although women bear the brunt of the effects of all of these, men share the responsibility and the fallout, too.

And then we will also make time to laugh and eat and go on outings, where we can get to know each other better and nurture each other and remind ourselves that God is a God of celebration and joy, not just of duty.

At the heart of all our discussions will be our times of worship and Bible study. We know ourselves to be most fundamentally true to ourselves as we are together in God's presence. The Lambeth Conference is not a parliament or UN gathering, but God's people, taking counsel together for God's mission.

What we hope for from the spouses' conference is most profoundly that we will get to know each other better. Christian ministry is incarnational. It matters that it is done by particular people in particular situations. It is meant to be done differently by different people with different gifts. It is not meant to be done by automata working with universal blueprints. So there is really no alternative to meeting and talking and praying together. That is the only way to appreciate what God is doing in the Anglican Church.

As a result of the spouses' conference, we hope to be able to pray for each other better. We hope we know where to turn to for expertise in particular areas. We hope to go home knowing that we are understood. We hope to face our differences with real pain because we love each other. We hope to laugh and cry and dance and sing and go home better equipped to do what God has given us to do. Above all, we hope to be reminded of the awesomeness of the God who has entrusted so much to us.

Friendship and respect are the currency of the Anglican Church. It does not have a single constitution or a single authority structure. If we do not know or trust each other, we cannot function. To some, that seems like the biggest weakness of Anglicanism, but I think it is our greatest strength. What other kind of a Church should there be? What other kind of Christians should there be?

At Lambeth 1998, unbreakable friendships were formed, friendships that have nurtured people and shaped their Christian discipleship ever since. Everyone who participated learned again the nature of our God, who calls people from every nation and of every kind to meet at his table and be fed. If Lambeth 2008 can do that, it will have fulfilled our hopes and it will equip us for the next ten years of challenging, hard and spectacular ministry.

Kaleidoscope

On the following pages, celebrating the diversity of bishops' spouses and their contributions to the life of the Church: Louise Morais-Neufville, Denise Inge, Lily Lai – three utterly different people, with vivid stories to tell and their own approach to the challenges and joys of being married to the Bishop.

Louise Morais-Neufville
Liberia (West Africa), married to
Rt Revd Edward Neufville

Unconsciously, I find myself acting as an administrative assistant to the Bishop because I am forced into the situation of advocating for people who want the Bishop to help them in some way or other. Most people in my diocese say, 'You are our mother, we are your children. We must cry to you first so that you can whisper it to the Bishop, he will listen to you.' Sometimes I feel that I am trespassing when I do, but the Bishop does not make me feel that way. However, I have tried to let the Bishop be the Bishop by limiting my interventions.

The work of a bishop is fraught with pressures and tensions and there is no way the spouse can avoid feeling those pressures. Much of the time the spouse becomes the Bishop's chaplain, counsellor, advisor and pacifier. When he comes home and unloads his problems before you, you also take them on, so you share the burden. It is a heavy, lonely and daily task. What I learned in all of this is that you are, most of the time, the counsellor and pacifier but no one counsels you. It is a lonely feeling.

As wife of a bishop, there is a tendency on the part of the people not to allow you to be yourself. Their expectations are so high that to express your anger, displeasure or emotions is far below their expectation. The Bishop's wife is to remain calm and serene at all times. Even if she is hurting, people will raise an eyebrow if it is the reverse.

The wife of a bishop is an ordinary lay person who must be allowed the freedom to be just that. She is not a trained liturgist nor a theologian nor a specialist in parish administration. She learns and grows and matures in her husband's ministry. In some dioceses, the wife of the Bishop is expected to take the lead in most church activities – head of the Mothers' Union, head of the Girls' Friendly Society, etc.

In my diocese (Diocese of Liberia), the Episcopal Church women expect the active involvement of the Bishop's wife in church activities as advisor, but not necessarily to head organizations. Here, some latitude of choice-making is allowed. In the Clergy Wives Association, the Bishop's wife is always the president of the Association and other clergy wives are voted on to or elected to other positions.

My experience tells me that the Bishop's wife stands on the same social pedestal as her husband; this requires the exercise of utmost care in her behaviour in the community so as not to damage the image of the Bishop and that of the diocese.

Let us remember that the Bishop's detractors are also those of his spouse. The challenge is that the Bishop's spouse remains a role model always. In my setting, the Bishop's wife serves as a liaison between the Bishop and the parishioners. Because people look up to the Bishop's wife that way, the temptation is to keep going without allowing oneself some time to rest, just because you care; so I have learned that if you allow yourself to be used, so be it.

On the other hand, I enjoyed my ministry as a bishop's wife especially in the rural area where my husband was assigned to provide oversight for the northern archdeaconry, when he was suffragan bishop. That area was virgin and ripe for evangelism as the majority of the population was not exposed to Christianity. Most of them were subsistence farmers who left their children to roam the village and fend for themselves while their parents left for their farms to work till late evening. I used that opportunity to gather the abandoned children in a small unfinished house and taught them the ABCs, nursery rhymes, Bible stories and some songs. This effort grew into a small school and church, which have become the only Episcopal school and Episcopal church in that community.

My husband was elected diocesan bishop in the middle of the fifteen-year ravaging civil war in our country. I had to be mother to the diocese. The entire membership was severely traumatized and deprived of their material possessions, parents, children and other family members. As a bishop's wife, I was no exception to the toll of the war because we lost our house to mortar explosions and our clothes and other possessions to the rebels. We were also traumatized. Yet I was looked up to to deliver some relief when I was myself a candidate for assistance. The feeling of inadequacy to help was depressing and frustrating. But God being so great, I tried to mobilize some small support and handouts from friends in the United States. Also as the wife of a bishop, people always expect you to have to deliver even if you cannot afford to do so. People think your resources never run out.

One other thing I have learned during my ten years as a diocesan bishop's wife is that people who borrow from you, be it money or any other item, find it difficult to repay most of the time. A loan is no different from a gift, only because people carry the notion that the Bishop's wife is wealthy.

As the Bishop's wife you are the mother to all parishioners, mother to the priests and to their wives as well. The challenge is that you have to always be there for them in their bereavements, family problems or other situations. All must be embraced and enjoy your moral and spiritual support.

When I became a bishop's wife it was a big challenge for me to forgo my attachment to a particular parish and my small community of friends. To transit to the entire diocese as my parish was challenging. What happens, however, is that one's circle of friends is enlarged and not narrowed.

In Liberia, there is now only one diocese with one bishop and his wife. The challenge is that there is no other bishop's wife within my diocese to compare notes or even to discuss any pressing or burning issues with. One bishop's wife with several priests' wives looking up to her for guidance has a real challenge.

Denise Inge
Huntingdon (Ely Diocese, England; now Worcester, England), married to Rt Revd John Inge

I am a mother and a writer, an academic, a landlady, a gardener, a hostess, a visitor, a stranger and the wife of a bishop. Hardly any of these occupations pay well, none of them are dull, all have the capacity to surprise me. Most of what I do I do for love, a kind of jumbled love of God, my children, my husband, of words, of the country I live in, a love of the breathtakingly beautiful natural world, of the more general humankind my neighbour. I am a lucky one then, a person whose life, though a bit dishevelled, is largely composed of happily chosen hats worn in quick succession. Usually I have time to wash my hands between gardening and hostessing, or clearing drains and visiting, there may even be time for a quick splash of my current favourite perfume, Chanel *Chance*; but I have been known to be caught attending to the most basic needs of tiny children while answering the phone call from tenants (phone under my chin), cleaning a trowel, and composing the next chapter of a book in my head at the same time. At times like that, the really hard thing is getting the sticky front door to open. Oh, and remembering the name of the person on the other side of it.

My problem, you see, is that I keep forgetting I *am* the wife of a bishop – that there are things, like names, I *ought* to know, things I ought to *do* and ought *not* to do. Like popping out quickly to the shops on your bike in your shorts on a hot summer day (whoops, forgot that one last year and I still remember the looks in this small cathedral 'city'). Maybe it is because we do not live in a palace. If I lived in a proper bishop's palace with enormous rooms and everlasting staircases I might be reminded every time I went out and home again, even every time I tried to find my pair of scissors, that the reason it took me ten minutes to track down a hunted object was the vastness of my house, the importance of my husband and the role I too had to inhabit. But you see, that just doesn't happen in my practical 1930s pebble-dashed suburban dream home. Life inside this house looks really pretty normal. Our domestic arrangements are neat, efficient and completely adequate. In spite of that, and of all the socially more correct connotations of my present situation, I find myself rather wishing we did live in such a palace. The socially responsible in me knows I shouldn't, but another side of me longs to see preserved and used what is ancient and hospitable, noble and beautiful. Offering hospitality is a joy to me. It would be so lovely to be able to really spoil people with an invitation to somewhere gracious and interesting.

What do I do all day? We have two delicious daughters – $2^1/_2$ and 7 – who are perhaps my most lasting work. I spend a good deal of my time in the day-to-day of ballet and piano lessons, playgroup and potty training, the practical prayers of motherhood and the litany of laundry (what goes in dirty comes out clean; some stains need a bit more bleaching in the sun, the mismatched are paired, the rent mended, the lost retrieved). Three precious mornings a week I also savour the book-blessed air of libraries, pore over ancient manuscripts, and write about a wise seventeenth-century priest named Thomas Traherne who believed that God's world is essentially good, that we humans, made for happiness, are 'as prone to love as the sun is to shine', and that the true treasures are those things most common, simple and useful – radical statements in our terror threatened, ecologically foreboding, and deeply consumerist age. To fund these impecunious passions, my children and my work, and in order to provide an eventual home for us when, in retirement, we are finally turfed out of palaces (real or imagined) for ever, I also play the landlady – furnishing, finding tenants, paying bills, repairing, maintaining, clearing drains, changing light bulbs, keeping abreast of endless new government health and safety initiatives – ho hum. Gardening I do for the sheer joy of it. Soil through my fingers, birdsong in my ears, the scent of earth and the scent of roses, ashes to ashes, dust to dust – there the clear spearhead of a *colchea* piercing the bare earth; even in autumn resurrection. I pick apples, gather twigs for the bonfire, spend six times as long as it would take me to peel supermarket carrots peeling knobbly ones because our hopeful daughter grew them.

There are bishops' wives in other places who forage their food among roots. There are those in countries antipathetic to Christianity and intolerant in the extreme whose husbands' hands may be cut off if they dare to baptize openly. I know of one who learned to fly a plane so she could get her husband around his vast

Australian diocese. These women shame me with their amazing strength, resilience and fortitude. My trivial discontents and yawning complacencies alike sting like a bed of nettles. Theirs are the lives we should know about, their stories the ones likely to inspire. But I cannot tell them.

I said I was a stranger. That is true. Born an American and raised there, but settled now in England, I have become a sojourner. Treated kindly by an English culture that is tolerant enough to accept without remonstrance the eccentricity of my birth, though it cannot fill the voids present in my particular cultural experience, I am also now a stranger to an America whose pace of change long ago outstripped my case of memories. Belonging here and nowhere, more making a home than being at home. I re-belong everywhere we move, never knowing where we will end up. 'We' I write since I can scarcely imagine where I would belong without him. This confession is as scary as it is soppy, but it may have a place in a book that is, after all (I shudder – are we really to be defined and gathered in terms as arbitrary as this connection with a dominant male?), looking at the lives of wives.

'How do you like being a bishop's wife?' people often ask (as if there were someone else whose wife I might be instead). 'Well,' I want to reply, though I don't since it would make him sound rather like a piece of cheese, 'I wouldn't want to be any other bishop's wife, but I like being married to this one.' I know they are just making conversation, but it is a question I really don't know how to answer. I mean, it seems to me either you are happy in your skin or you are not – whether your husband is the Bishop of Huntingdon, the tailor down the street, or the Grand Poobah of Mishikoto. I think what they are getting at is something deeper that neither they nor I articulate. Something about the marriage of public roles and private lives, something about tiny local celebrity, maybe even something about living a life connected to divine purpose. And there is something real in that. There is a certain weight in any public office. There are binding confidences. There are whole spheres where utmost discretion must be exercised. There are privileges. There are responsibilities. But don't many people experience these to some degree in their work or in their family life?

What is seriously different about being a bishop's wife (or any priest's wife for that matter) is that you are married to someone who belongs to God. To the Church, to other people, more deeply than either of you can say. This, at the end of the day, not the palace (or absence of one), nor the glittering invitations (pleasant though they be), nor the small demands and intrusions that come your way, is what being married to a bishop means. I expect it means this in every culture and in every time. He is never yours. Parts of him, yes, sometimes the best bits, sometimes the leftovers. But he is never wholly yours. Being a bishop's wife, in the end, has little to do with the status or role of either of you. It has to do with this God-shaped place that is in each of us and that he happens to have been called to articulate in a particular and public manner. For some bishops' wives this means huge and costly sacrifices. I am one of the lucky ones. So little is required of me, and what I do I mostly do for love. But there are times when I do not accidentally forget I am a bishop's wife.

On Christmas morning, for instance, the children pounce on the bed and you all open stockings and then, instead of descending upon the parcels waiting round the tree below, he puts on the uniform, untangles himself from the clinging arms of children and off he goes to a prison full of sex offenders where neither you nor the girls can follow. You know that this, though it flies in the face of every other family's routine across the country, though it leaves you lonely and hassled (of all days Christmas), your children frustrated, everyone halted in the midst of celebration and the fizz of excitement spoiling, is what he was born for and what, deep down, you believe in. It was probably, truth to tell, why you married him – because you wanted to stay near the heart of the gospel. You stuff the turkey and stitch it closed with a fat needle and stout thread like your mother used to, hoping that the tiny shard of ice in your heart will melt, as icicles do in the midday sun. In the prison chapel there are men in mitres and boiler suits singing. About the time you put the roast potatoes in he will have started the rounds in the truly gruesome isolation unit. About the time the children ask for the third time when will Daddy be home, he will be walking through disinfectant in the cells where prisoners in the midst of dirty protests wait for the clear white host his hands bring. Or shout obscenities in rage. 'Not long now,' you say, the icicle at its finest point. What will be left? A small pool of water, thank God. Simple, common and useful.

Lily Lai
Taiwan (part of the Episcopal Church of the USA), married to Rt Revd David Lai

Most people in Taiwan follow the traditional folk-religion practices of Taoism mixed with Buddhism, and my family was no exception. My father and mother were very devout in their daily ancestor worship and in their prayers to the gods. From the start they opposed me going to church or having anything to do with Christianity. It is only by the grace of God that I can write these words now, as I look back on my journey to faith and its most unlikely and seemingly impossible start.

When I was 9 years old, the local Presbyterian church started a children's outreach programme on the street outside our home in Tainan, south-west Taiwan. Every Saturday afternoon I would take my youngest sister (then aged 2) outside to listen to the evangelist preaching the gospel. My mother did not like this, and one day when it rained we ran home soaked, only to get a beating from my mother!

My father was a police officer and was sent to work on the east coast of Taiwan, so I moved with one of my sisters to my grandmother's house. Several of my classmates were Christians, and they often shared the gospel with me and invited me to go with them to church activities. One day a missionary came to our house and invited me to kneel down and pray, so I did. My grandmother was so angry. When my mother returned to visit us and discovered I was going along to church, she beat me again!

Family life changed dramatically when my father had an affair and moved out to live with this new woman. My mother was very angry and blamed me. It was because she was pregnant with me that she had to get married in the first place, so she saw it as my fault that she was in this mess now. My mother decided that I should have no more education, but should get a job. My father on the other hand supported me in my desire to complete my education, so I moved to live with him and his girlfriend. At that time I was the best student in Tainan High School for Girls, but my father lived in Kaohsiung. So each day I would wake up at 4 a.m., prepare my lunch box, walk one hour to the station, catch the first train to Tainan and then walk thirty-five minutes to the school. Each day I had to pass the river which was reputed to be full of ghosts, and I would sing choruses and hymns to get me safely past!

My father's girlfriend didn't like me studying and told my father I wanted to stop my education and look for a job. So she tried to tempt me to become a dancing girl in one of the dancing halls. For two months in the summer vacation I worked there selling tickets, each night returning home on foot after midnight. These dancing halls were run by the local mafia and had a bad reputation. I was so afraid of what might happen to me and I used to sing choruses to help calm me. Eventually I told my father, and he gave me some money and told me to leave the house and move away. But where could I go? I eventually ended up living in a convent near my school. Things were fine until the convent needed all the rooms for a retreat and I was homeless once more.

Fortunately I heard that Grace Episcopal Church in Tainan had a hostel and I moved there. That was my first contact with the Episcopal Church. The priest there at that time, John Chien, was later to become Bishop of Taiwan, but my first memory is of him banging on my door while I was hiding inside, too afraid to answer! He needed me to help him take care of his wife, who had just had a baby, so I helped wash the vegetables and prepare the food for her. That first day helping them, I also met my future husband for the first time! At that time David was at Tainan Theological College, and assigned to Grace Church for field work. It was Chinese New Year and David's family were too far away for him to return home, so he spent the time with John and Grace Chien. Grace invited me to go to church that Sunday, and kept on inviting me week after week. Through their witness, care and encouragement, I was eventually baptized and became a committed Christian.

My testimony is one of amazing grace. Despite all the opposition, temptations and difficulties of my early life, God has proved faithful to me and showed me he is indeed the way, the truth and the life. When David was elected Bishop of Taiwan to succeed Bishop John Chien, in the year 2000, we already had good role models to follow. I was able to retire from my teaching post and we moved to Taipei to start our new ministry. I do whatever I can to help David, I am more than willing to support him. I am the supervisor for one of our church kindergartens, and I have a particular ministry among clergy wives and the female members of our churches. There is a lot of prayer, counselling and encouragement needed to help these wonderful women in their journey of faith and their outreach to others.

Before, we took care of one small church; now we have a whole diocese. We also work on building relationships with other denominations in Taiwan, with other dioceses in ECUSA (of which we are a part), as well as other dioceses in Asia. We share a vision to be a bridge between the churches in Asia and the USA, and to promote reconciliation between those who think differently, that we may be able to work together for the good of God's Kingdom.